Women Living the Psalms

Women Living the Psalms

A Guide to Everyday Spirituality

KAREN KAIGLER-WALKER

WIPF & STOCK · Eugene, Oregon

WOMEN LIVING THE PSALMS
A Guide to Everyday Spirituality

Copyright © 2025 Karen Kaigler-Walker. All rights reserved. Except for brief quotations in critical publications or reviews, no part of this book may be reproduced in any manner without prior written permission from the publisher. Write: Permissions, Wipf and Stock Publishers, 199 W. 8th Ave., Suite 3, Eugene, OR 97401.

Wipf & Stock
An Imprint of Wipf and Stock Publishers
199 W. 8th Ave., Suite 3
Eugene, OR 97401

www.wipfandstock.com

PAPERBACK ISBN: 979-8-3852-2131-8
HARDCOVER ISBN: 979-8-3852-2132-5
EBOOK ISBN: 979-8-3852-2133-2

Where indicated, Scripture is quoted from the New Revised Standard Version, Updated Edition. Copyright © 2021 National Council of Churches of Christ in the United States of America. Used by permission. All rights reserved worldwide.

Where indicated, Scripture is quoted from the Christian Standard Bible. Copyright © 2017 by Holman Bible Publishers. Used by permission. Christian Standard Bible®, and CSB® are federally registered trademarks of Holman Bible Publishers, all rights reserved.

AKJV: Authorized (King James) Version
ASV: American Standard Version
ISV: International Standard Version
CEB: Common English Version
CEBW: Common English Version Women's Bible
CSB: Christian Standard Bible
ESVUK: English Standard Version Anglicized
ESV: English Standard Version
GNT: Good News Translation
ISV: International Standard Version
KJ21: 21st Century King James Version
KJV: King James Version
MEV: Modern English Version
MSG: Message
NABRE: New American Bible, Revised Edition
NASB: New American Standard Bible
NET: New English Translation
NIV: New International Version
NIVUK: New International Version United Kingdom
NJB: New Jerusalem Bible
NKJV: New King James Version
NLT: New Living Translation
NRSV: New Revised Standard Version
NRSVue: New Revised Standard Version Updated Version
NRSVA: New Revised Standard Version Anglicized
PHB: Peshitta Holy Bible
REB: Revised English Bible
RSV: Revised Standard Version
TLB: The Living Bible
VOICE: The Voice

Women Living the Psalms is dedicated to my sisters in Christ, those whom I know, those whom I've taught, those who've read my books, and those whom I've not yet met. We're a strong sisterhood, yearning to live in God daily.

The psalmists beseeched God, praised God, spoke to God, and raged at God, emptying their emotions of fear, anger, joy, and gratitude regarding what was going on in their daily lives. In communicating closely, one-on-one with God, they cut through the need for theologies, rituals, and creeds. Although they turned to God as their trusted benefactor with whom they could converse freely, their relationship remained as loving subjects to the One whom they worshiped.

Table of Contents

Acknowledgments | ix

Introduction | 3
My Story | 17

PART I: *Praise: Worship, Adoration, Acclamation, and Tribute*

Chapter 1 Psalm 145 | 29
Chapter 2 Psalm 146 | 32
Chapter 3 Psalm 63 | 34
Chapter 4 Psalm 40 | 36
Chapter 5 Psalm 8 | 39
Chapter 6 Psalm 89 | 41
Chapter 7 Psalm 121 | 45

PART II: *Assurance: Trust, Safety, Help, and Confidence in God*

Chapter 8 Psalm 125 | 53
Chapter 9 Psalm 16 | 55
Chapter 10 Psalm 54 | 59
Chapter 11 Psalm 62 | 61
Chapter 12 Psalm 20 | 64
Chapter 13 Psalm 9 | 66

Part III: *Thanksgiving: Gratitude, Joy, and Blessings*

Chapter 14 Psalm 95 | 74
Chapter 15 Psalm 100 | 76

Table of Contents

Chapter 16 Psalm 138 | 77
Chapter 17 Psalm 92 | 79
Chapter 18 Psalm 136 | 81
Chapter 19 Psalm 30 | 84
Chapter 20 Psalm 105 | 86

PART IV: *Lament: Loss Pain, Grief, Fear, Questioning God, and Anger*

Chapter 21 Psalm 13 | 96
Chapter 22 Psalm 130 | 98
Chapter 23 Psalm 6 | 101
Chapter 24 Psalm 38 | 104
Chapter 25 Psalm 10 | 107
Chapter 26 Psalm 22 | 110

PART V: *Wisdom: Guidance, Grace, and Understanding*

Chapter 27 Psalms 51 | 120
Chapter 28 Psalm 1 | 123
Chapter 29 Psalm 37 | 125
Chapter 30 Psalm 111 | 128
Chapter 31 Psalm 19 | 130
Chapter 32 Psalm 112 | 133

PART VI: *Kinship*

Chapter 33 Psalm 119 | 137

PART VII: *Conclusion*

Chapter 34 Psalm 91 | 152
Chapter 35 Psalm 23 | 156

Benediction | 161
Epilogue | 163
Activities for Individuals and Groups | 165
Bibliography | 169

Acknowledgments

My first debt of gratitude is to my husband, Bud Walker. To say that it's not easy being married to a writer is an understatement of the grandest order. Often, I'm moody, and oftentimes that's an understatement. Thank you for the love and support, even through the disappointments I've caused you and the too many times when you've had to shop for and cook your own dinner. I owe you!

I couldn't have written the book without my bestie, Zelda Gilbert, my cheerleader and soft place to land when I needed one. Oh, how you can make me laugh at the right time, Dr. Z. My world wouldn't be as blessed without you.

A *huge* thank you to my friends, readers, and Facebook followers—too many to mention individually—who supported me through the ups and downs over the past year, from the inception and naming of *Living the Psalms* to the day I submitted the final manuscript to Wipf and Stock. I'm especially grateful for my sisters in the United Methodist Women (UMW) of the First Methodist Church of Fort Worth, my UMW Hannah Circle sisters, and members of the Texas Horizon Conference of the United Women in Faith (formerly UMW). Then there are the women at the Retreat House and Spirituality Center in Richardson, Texas, who've encouraged my writing over the past several years. You're great!

I'm grateful for those who read early editions and endorsed the book: Wendy Campbell, president of the United Women of Faith, Horizon Texas Conference, United Methodist Church (UMC); Rev. Thomas Long, district superintendent of the Horizon

Acknowledgments

Texas Conference of the United Methodist Church UMC; Rev. Linda McDermott, associate pastor (retired) of the First UMC, Fort Worth; Rev. Dr. Lilian Smith, co-founder of the Retreat House Spirituality Center, Richardson, Texas; and Julie K. Rhodes, Christian author and friend.

Finally, I thank the men and women at Wipf and Stock Publishers for their faith and trust in me to write *Living the Psalms*. I'm especially thankful to Matthew Weimer for his patience and guidance. When I say I couldn't have done it without him, it's true. I neither would nor could have.

Let the words of my mouth and the meditation of my heart
be acceptable to you, O Lord, my rock and my redeemer. (Ps 19:14)

Introduction

IN A 2014 SERMON, Rev. Dr. Otis Moss III told this story: "My father asked an elder woman in his congregation, 'How are you doing, Mother?' She replied, 'I'm living between "Oh Lord" and "Thank you, Jesus."'" He goes on, "For the most part, many of us are living in between, not quite at 'Oh Lord' and not quite at 'Thank you, Jesus,' but somewhere in between."[1]

When I read this, I didn't know whether to laugh or cry. So, I did a little of both. As women, that's how we live. Some days it's "Oh Lord." We get a call from the doctor we never wanted to receive. It breaks us. "Oh God!" At another time, when God has answered our most fervent prayers, and we see two pink lines after years of tries and failures, we go to our knees and cry, "Thank you, Jesus!" As Rev. Moss mentioned, most of the time we toggle somewhere in between small joys and annoyances. Maybe we find what we've been searching for on Google immediately—"Yay God!" Then there are days we get our knickers in a knot because we're running late and the school pickup line is as long as it's ever been. "Why now?"

Moss's[2] story also reminds me of the psalmists of old who reached out to the Holy One and poured out their hearts about what was going on in their lives by crying "O Lord" or "Thank You, God." Theirs were neither amorphous pleas and praises to a distant or formal god nor mere hopes that God might hear and respond.

1. Moss III, "Gospel and the Blues."
2. Onwuchekwa, *We Go On*, loc. 141 of 260.

Their songs and prayers were personal and intimate. The psalmists called God *Yahweh*, which comes from the verb "to be"—a living, acting God, a loving companion, and a friend to whom they could lay out what was in the deepest part of their hearts. We're no different today.

Gabby Cudjoe-Wilkes and Andrew Wilkes affirm this: "The Psalms are rediscovered with fresh eyes by every generation. They speak across differences in cultures, social contexts, and even centuries. The Psalms are beloved for their emotional rawness, their urge toward justice, and their blunt candor about the coarse edges of a life spent walking with God."[3]

UNIQUENESS OF *PSALMS*

Bible trivia time. Did you know that the book of Psalms is the only book written to God in a personal way? I didn't until I started researching for this book. No wonder it's so well loved. In *We Go On*, John Onwuchekwa wrote, "I've heard someone say that while the rest of the Bible speaks to us, the Psalms speak for us."[4] "Thank you, God."

The psalmists beseeched God, praised God, spoke to God, and raged at God, emptying their emotions of fear, anger, joy, and gratitude to God regarding what was going on in their daily lives. In this close, one-on-one conversation with God, they cut through the need for theologies, rituals, and creeds.

God is addressed by name 695 times in the Hebrew Bible (Old Testament), all of them representing this personal yet worship-filled relationship with the Almighty. In Ps 91:1–2 alone, God is addresses as *'Elyôwn* (most High), *Shaddai* (most Almighty), *Jehovah* (I am the one who is), and *'Elōhîm* (godhood). Later, in the New Testament, Jesus calls God *Abba*, a common or everyday term for a respected father that expressed affection, confidence, and trust.

---

3. Cudjoe-Wilkes and Wilkes, *Psalms for Black Lives*, loc. 70 of 196.
4. Onwuchekwa, *We Go On*, loc. 140 of 260.

INTRODUCTION

It's the same with us today. We are blessed by God first to be able to develop this loving and close relationship, and second, we are taught how to communicate with God through the psalms. Quoting my seminary professor, Dr. John Goldingay, Nancy L. deClaisse-Walford et al. write:

> John Goldingay has aptly put it, the "Psalms make it possible to say things that are otherwise unsayable." At times the psalms give us words to express anguish that we cannot bring ourselves to express. At other times they allow us to express the joy we feel, but to do so in a theological register [acceptable way]. And at still other times, we do not sing them because they say or feel what we already believe or feel, but because by speaking them we can come to believe what they say, feel what they feel, and trust where they trust.[5]

As if offering us a guide to interact with God personally, intimately, and about our daily lives weren't enough, often we find God answering the psalmists with reassurances. We'll explore this more later, but for now, it's important to note God's active role because it assures us that God listens to and responds to us.

I thought of this when I read the following in Sarah Bessy's *Miracles and Other Reasonable Things*:

> I need—then and now—the God who sits in the mud and in the cold wind, in the laundry pile and in the city park, who is as present in homework and nightly baths and homemade meals and hospital rooms and standing by caskets. I need a God with teeth and hunger, who embodies grief and joy; wisdom and patience; renewal with simplicity and a good, deep breath; and who even now shows up in the unlikeliest and homeliest of lives too, as a sacrament and a blessing for the ordinary incarnation of feet on the ground and baptism of the water and wings wide in the sky. I have come to love the mud and the reeds, the water and the quiet day, just as much as the feel of the wind in my hair as I take flight and soar.[6]

---

5. deClaisse-Walford et al., *Book of Psalms*, loc. 422 of 3784.
6. Bessy, *Miracles*, loc. 278 of 2636.

I add to that my need for that God of the "everyday" when I'm a flipping wreck and my mind is so muddled I can't think my way out of a room with an open door. Perhaps that's when I need God most because at these times, I'm incapable of moving, much less moving forward.

When I teach classes on psalms, I get this idea of "everydayness" across by using the example of when Sir Charles Spencer called his sister, Diana, the princess of Wales, the "peoples' princess" at her funeral. Think of the book of Psalms as the "peoples' verses." They are metaphors for our everyday need for God to us direct to where we need to go in mind, heart, and body with comfort, confirmation, and assurance.

It's no wonder the book of Psalms is the favorite, most loved, and most read book in the Hebrew and Christian Bibles. Many of us learned the Twenty-Third Psalm in Sunday school, and it remains the go-to psalm among Jews and Christians as we age. Many non-Jews and non-Christians also love it for its promise that all will be well and that we can carry on no matter what. How many times did we hear it quoted after 9/11 by people of every stripe?

OUR LOVE AFFAIR WITH THE PSALMS

In *Getting Involved with God*, Psalms scholar Ellen F. Davis tells us, "The Psalms are about: speaking our mind honestly and fully before God. The Psalms are a kind of First Amendment for the faithful. They guarantee us complete freedom of speech before God, and then (something no secular constitution would ever do) they give us a detailed model of how to exercise that freedom, even up to its dangerous limits, to the very brink of rebellion."[7] Davis wrote this in 2001, long before Christian nationalism moved front and center. Thus, I caution you about using her words as a cornerstone of your beliefs in this area. That would be using them out of context in a way she didn't intend, based on reading her entire book.

---

7. Davis, *Getting Involved with God*, loc. 193 of 413.

INTRODUCTION

Davis goes on, "The Psalter is the one book of the Bible to which, it seems, prayerful Christians require *immediate daily access* [italics mine]. They are even there at the back of my tiny traveler's edition of the New Testament, the kind that evangelistic shopkeepers distribute free to their customers."[8] This reminds me that Psalms is included in the tiny white leather New Testament my parents gave me when I was baptized. After I read Davis's words, I pulled the wee book, now yellowed with age but not quite brittle, out of storage and keep it on the chest in our guest bedroom.

She writes, "Of course, there is a reason why they are ubiquitous, and why we should begin with them: because the Psalms are the single best guide to the spiritual life currently in print. They will likely still be on the shelf long after everything else in the spirituality section of the bookstore has gone out of print. Anything you could learn from the other books is already there, at least in kernel form, in the Psalter."[9]

Before moving on to why and how we live the psalms, let's look at one more plus in their corner—one I wasn't aware of until I read Melannie Svoboda's *Traits of a Healthy Spirituality*: "[The Psalms] celebrate the dignity of the human person: 'Yet you have made them [us humans] a little lower than God, and crowned them with glory and honor.'"[10] Wow! Did that ever grab me by the soul!

So, when David penned "He restoreth my soul" (Ps 23:3 KJV), he was recognizing that God breathes our Godlike selves back into us to make us whole when we are dry. Dominic Done puts it this way: "He will return my breath to me. That's what we long for, isn't it? Our truest self is screaming for air, desperate to break through the surface of a shallow, hurried life and breathe deeply of God himself. To exhale failure and inhale grace. To come alive again."[11] Amen, Brother Dominic!

---

8. Davis, *Getting Involved with God*, loc. 121 of 413.
9. Davis, *Getting Involved with God*, loc. 193 of 413.
10. Svoboda, *Traits*, loc. 372 of 2824.
11. Done, *Your Longing*, 27.

LIVING THE PSALMS

When asking "How do we live the psalms?," I'm talking about *really* living them so they inform our thinking and doing no matter what's going on, not just reading, contemplating, or reciting them so we can either check them off our reading list for the week or hope to remember them when needed. For when the psalmists wrote their songs and the people sang them, they were present with God, focused on God, and understood well that God was the ground of their being *in all things at all times*.

Personally, turning to the psalms is the best way for me to stay grounded when I don't know where I'm going, what I am trying to achieve, or faced with problems that seem insurmountable. In these times we can feel small and ineffective, even stagnated, which pushes us into a mild case of despondency or into full-blown depression. If we've learned to lean on the words of the psalmists, we automatically bring God into the situation to help, support, and guide us, as well as help us praise, worship, thank, and share joy with him.

For example, Ps 63, written by David when he was a fugitive in the wilderness of Judah, fearing for his life, shows us how we can address God in our darkest hours, bless God, be grateful to God in joy, and be assured that God will help us. We'll discuss Ps 63 in depth in chapter 3.

Inasmuch as Ps 63 speaks to our deepest emotions, let's break the habit of thinking that the psalms are there for us only in high times of panic, pain, or joy. I was reading along in Alua Arthur's *Briefly Perfectly Human* when I came across her description of being lonely one day when she couldn't point to why, "aside from my poor decision-making, my aimlessness, and the depression coating my brain like a cloudy lacquer finish."[12] "That's me sometimes," I thought. I have days like this—another good reason to turn to psalms such as Ps 119:105 (KJV): "Your word is a lamp unto my feet."

---

12. Arthur, *Briefly Perfectly Human*, 402.

Introduction

BENEFITS OF LIVING THE PSALMS

Blogger and devotional writer Stacey Salsbery recently posted "20 Benefits of Being in God's Word According to Psalm 119," a single song that covers all the main benefits in Psalms.[13]

1. Leading us to joy.
2. Keeping us from going our own way without God.
3. Offering free counseling.
4. Guarding us against the trap of self-seeking.
5. Giving us hope.
6. Granting us freedom.
7. Bringing comfort in affliction.
8. Giving us something to sing and shout about.
9. Offering an anchor in God's truth.
10. Encouraging and showing us how to be an example to others.
11. Offering hope while we wait.
12. Sustaining us during hard seasons.
13. Providing life-giving options.
14. Giving us wisdom and understanding.
15. Lighting the path we should take.
16. Keeping us from falling into dangerous traps.
17. Acting as a shield around us.
18. Helping us know the nature of God.
19. Showing us how to experience the faithfulness of God.
20. Giving us peace.

In addition to Salsbery's, I'll add five more benefits. First, they can impart deep meaning or give a lift for the day, depending on what we need. If we read them often and strive to live in them

---

13. Salsbery, "20 Benefits."

more deeply, over time, rereading them or remembering them will help us trust God even more to support us in whatever way we need, thereby enabling us to handle whatever situation we're in, whether it be pain or joy.

Second, psalms are multifaceted in that the same one can help us with various needs, emotional states, and life events. Often, we can even find that two or more psalms can be combined to help us work through a complicated situation to a satisfactory conclusion.

Third, earlier we talked about each generation reading psalms to suit what's going on in their world. Yet, the same psalms are for all ages as we move through our own life stages and help others through theirs. What comforted me in the Twenty-Third Psalm when I was a kid shifted as I became a teen, a young woman, a middle-aged woman, and an elder. It offered different understandings and takeaways. As I move into my final years, I know that its meaning will shift again. At the private family service the night before the public service for my cousin, Angela, I read the beloved KJV version of the Twenty-Third Psalm to carry her home.

When we get down to it, although generational, time, and cultural differences exist, our basic needs and concerns as women aren't totally generation-, time-, and/or culture-bound. Here, we close the loop. Living the psalms brings us together as women—together in our needs for God's support and guidance through our interconnected circles of life.

My long-time, long-distance friend Cathy Zoomed me at the crack of dawn, barely (if that) holding it together. A wee-hour-of-the-morning call from her sister let her know that their mom, who lives across the country, had had a stroke. A half hour later, her distraught daughter, a sophomore at a university in a state on the other side of the country, texted that she was dropping out of college and flying home because she "couldn't find herself." In less than an hour, Cathy was caught in a full-blown and seemingly impossible sandwich-generation crisis. We cried, we talked, and we laughed a little as we tried to make sensible plans that would work for all three. While my heart was breaking for her, it also was breaking for her mom and daughter. Each needed God. Although

Introduction

they are different in age, crises, and hoped-for outcomes, each needed comfort, assurance, and wisdom. "Even though I walk through the darkest valley, I fear no evil, for you are with me; your rod and your staff, they comfort me" (Ps 23:4 NRSV).

Fourth, the psalms help us develop the ability to see the larger picture, assuring us that we don't fall victim to believing we are the only ones who face what life gives us and having to handle it alone. While seeing the larger picture doesn't lessen our joys, thanksgiving, pain, and fears, it does put them into perspective. We see that in being one of God's daughters, we are sisters who experience or have experienced what we are going through and are here for another.

Finally, psalms remind us that God shows us how to reorient what's going on in our lives toward a new direction and outcome. Perhaps we are telling God, "I don't like, can't live with, feel blocked by, or am becoming angry at or agitated with" a situation. Maybe we want to lash out at, don't have the means to handle, or know where a situation is going and/or how it likely will end. In these situations, psalms help us ask, "God, is there a better way? Can I make a change and find a better ending?" This comes in handy for me when I finally hit the wall with someone or something and don't want to cause more frustration or pain.

Last winter, my friend Kayla, an experienced leader of women's health events and licensed Masters in Social Work (MSW), anguished about overseeing a one-day midlife retreat because of Jen, another member of the team's demand that she be given almost full control of what the group was planning. Jen had no training in midlife issues, yet she wasn't deterred. This wasn't the first time Jen had wanted an event to be her way or the highway. Well-meaning and godly, yes, but Jen was beyond over-the-top controlling. Every stage of the planning became a tug-of-war. One-on-one phone calls and texts outside the team extended into the night, where Jen grilled Kayla on each aspect of the project that Kayla presented and countered her judgment. She then gaslighted Kayla when Kayla brought Jen's issues to the group, making her look like she misunderstood what Jen had meant. Finally, mounting tension started affecting the other team members.

After a month of this, Kayla was wrecked, knowing that despite her best efforts, the project was doomed if something didn't change. As Jen was a friend from years back, Kayla stewed. Was her professional ability to provide a solid program worth her longtime friendship with Jen? Kayla prayed. What was God's thinking in this, knowing both her talents and Jen's deep-seated drive to control no matter what the workshop accomplished? Finally realizing that her questioning God's judgment was childish, she turned to Ps 32:7–9:

> You are a hiding place for me;
> you preserve me from trouble;
> you surround me with glad cries of deliverance. *Selah*
>
> I will instruct you and teach you the way you should go;
> I will counsel you with my eye upon you.
>
> Do not be like a horse or a mule, without understanding,
> whose temper must be curbed with bit and bridle,
> else it will not stay near you. (NRSVue, italics mine)

Following tears and several discussions with God, Kayla resigned from the committee in a way that hurt no one. Jen found a new director who would work with her comfortably, and Kayla had a good night's sleep for the first time since the issue arose. I have no idea how the workshop went, but that's not the point of the story. The point is that Kayla turned the issue over to God and heeded God's guidance she received in the psalm.

UNDERSTANDING THE PSALMS

On one level, psalms are easy to understand. Most kids who memorize the twenty-third in Sunday school can tell you in a heartbeat what it means. But to mine a psalms' deeper meanings, it helps to know a few things about it.

Introduction

Psalms are divided into a beginning, where the writer tells God what's on their mind; middle, where the author will pour out the issue to God; and end. In ending, the psalmist will conclude that God is both present and will handle the situation or God will answer as to how things will be dealt with. We will see this clearly when we discuss Ps 91 in the conclusion (my favorite psalm, by the way).

The psalms are written in metaphors and imagery that the people would understand, as is most poetry from the beginning of humankind to now. Is Frost talking about actual fences in his poem or the boundary we should set up between ourselves and others to foster good relationships?[14] Imagery in the psalms often includes known animals to represent enemies, harm, bravery, etc., as they do in Aesop's fables.

The psalmists used repetition make a point. In Ps 136, the phrase "for his steadfast love endures forever" is used twenty-five times in the twenty-six verses. This is the highest expression of importance and reassurance that God will prevail. We see this throughout the Bible.

Each psalm can stand alone, whereas most chapters and books in the Bible are part of integrated understandings that must be read together for theme, content, and context. The most egregious failure to read and use Scripture is plucking out verses and short passages as stand-alone concepts, then picking and choosing among them.

In interpreting psalms today, let's remember that the ancient Hebrews were a Bronze Age, warring people, living in a violent world. Thus, we need to interpret the violent content differently today, as metaphors. Our modern adaptation is the bloodbaths we see in movies, video games, and TV programs, where the good folks overcome the bad folks by blowing them to smithereens. These fantasies are not meant to be a blueprint for real life but serve to give us relief through visual metaphors we can understand. As Christians today, our mighty God will prevail for us, not

---

14. Frost, "Road Not Taken," 48–49.

by violence but through the power of love and grace exemplified in Jesus's life.

Unfortunately, there are a few who don't see them this way. True story: I was signing copies of *Positive Aging* at the *Los Angeles Times* Festival of Books back after it came out.[15] Publishers set up booths with their authors and new releases and the crowds wandered from booth to booth. I'm sitting there when a woman walked by, introduced herself as a former missionary, and said she, too, writes Christian books for women. When I asked her to describe her book, she said it's about how she prays the psalms, pleading for God to kill her ex-husband and his new wife. Thinking the book must be some sort of Anne Lamott-ish, tongue-in-cheek approach to her failed marriage, I chuckled. She was not amused. She was serious. Her husband left her for "the other woman," and she wanted God to avenge her pain by wiping them off the face of the earth as with the Hebrew enemies in the olden days. Assuming the betrayal had happened recently, I thought the book was a knee-jerk reaction. No, the breakup happened twenty years ago. The poor woman obviously suffered from severe mental health issues, but in her pain, she had misunderstood the meaning of the vindictiveness in the psalms.

Finally, the Psalms were written by agrarian people whose culture, ways of phrasing, and examples used likely aren't understood by us today. Even the latest translations can leave us wondering and in need of some unpacking. Here again, let's look at the Twenty-Third Psalm as an example:

> Even though I walk through the darkest valley,
> I fear no evil,
> for you are with me; your rod and your staff,
> They comfort me. (v. 4, NRSV)

Notice first David is referring to God's rod and staff, not his own. How many of us know how and why God's rod and staff could protect David? They were the defense weapons and supports shepherds used as they tended their sheep. The rod (a wooden pole)

---

15. See Kaigler-Walker, *Positive Aging*.

INTRODUCTION

steadied their feet as they walked on stony, brushy, and uneven ground. It also helped them clear the way for the sheep and defend them from snakes and other dangers. The staff (crook) was used to pull the sheep out of snares, off ledges, and out of holes. So, when David referenced them, he was praising God for using God's tools (metaphorically) to protect him from the snares of evil and from going off God's path. Jesus referenced this understanding when he asked Peter to "tend my sheep" (John 21:16 NRSVue)—to "keep my people safe and on the path that I've prepare for them after my death."

CATEGORIES OF PSALMS

Being the longest book in the Bible with 150 songs compiled in no particular order, over the years, categories have been created based on major themes. A few, such as Ps 119, contain all themes. Most include a major theme and subthemes, and a few have only one theme.

For our purposes, we'll look at five categories based on this mnemonic that's helped untold Sunday school kids and freshmen in religion classes remember them.[16]

>   Praise (including joy)
>   Song of confidence and trust
>   ThAnksgiving
>   Lament
>   WisdoM
>   KinShip

HOW TO READ THIS BOOK

Like the psalms themselves, *Women Living the Psalms* can be read and reread, either in part or straight through, depending on your need and interest. I've made it easy for you to go directly to how

---

16. Postif, "Categorizing the Psalms."

and for what purpose you want to interact with God by dividing the book into parts. Looking for a lift? Read Part III, and so on.

Women Living the Psalms also can be used as a devotional, whereby you read and contemplate on one chapter at a time, straight through from cover to cover, and/or as a guide for individual or group study. For this, I included guidelines for individuals and groups at the end of the book. In certain instances, I've included points to ponder in the individual chapters. However you use it, I pray the book will draw you closer to God, increase your trust in God, and become more confident in God as you live in joy, pain, confusion, doubt, anger, and love daily.

The next section is an account of my life during the first six months of 2024. Although what happened to me was not overly profound in terms of what can happen to someone, it knocked me to my physical, emotional, and spiritual knees. Before it was over, I'd fervently prayed the full six types of the psalms discussed above.

My Story

> Give ear to my prayer, O God;
> do not hide yourself from my supplication.
> Attend to me and answer me;
> I am troubled in my complaint.
> I am distraught. (Ps 55:1–2 NRSVue)

IN FEBRUARY 2024, WITHIN 24 hours I careened between "Oh, God" and "Thank you, Jesus" so often I lost count. For the next four months, living the psalms rescued me from the worst physical and spiritual calamity in my life. I'm telling it as an example, not because of its uniqueness but because of how living various psalms guided my way through it, leaning on them as I moved from one stage to the next. For to really live the Psalms, they must be a seamless part of our thoughts, actions, and spirituality, no matter our condition.

This all began a week before Christmas 2023. Paying no mind whatsoever to what I was doing, when I reached the landing of a short set of stairs in our house, I saw Jackie, our imp of a shih tzu, running towards me with a sock in her mouth. Knowing she and the sock would whiz by me in a half second and thinking I was on the bottom step, I bent down to grab the sock so I wouldn't have to find it and bring it back up later. To get a better angle, I stepped back and leaned over. Before I could grab the sock, I fell backwards two steps. Going down hard, I realized I hadn't been on the landing but two steps up. Stunned, yet seemingly only a little hurt, I thought, "My bad," and pulled my aching self up.

"Oh, God!" Two hours later I was home from the ER in bed with a concussion, a broken rib, massive contusions on my right shoulder and elbow, and my back out of line. Several days later, I could hardly use my wrist. Christmas was different that year, but these things happen, I reckoned. Stupid me for not knowing where my feet were. Overall, the fall and its aftermath could have been much worse. "Thank you, Jesus."

The accident didn't upset me much other than having to stay in bed and cancel activities while my bestie, Zelda, was there for her annual Christmas/Hanukkah visit. Plus, the old trooper, me, didn't think the injuries were all *that* serious. Sure enough—thank you, Jesus—after a couple of weeks of staying down, I could use my computer and think clearly enough to finish the proposal for this book and submit to my publisher.

Despite the fall, in January, I was able to hobble to a women's retreat on body and soul care and then conducted another one. I went to meetings and other events, albeit coming home and heading to my office to nap. Two ibuprofens combined with a Tylenol at breakfast (what I called my "pain twins") and again at dinner got me by. I continued to post on my Facebook blog so my 18,000-plus followers would receive their daily soul care message from me. In other words, I never slowed down. I just hobbled, groaned, and medicated until I felt better.

Two weeks into February, I tumbled again, bouncing my head off a wall and landing (again) on my right side. This time I went down asking, "Oh God, what's with me?" Back in bed (again), I thought, "Karen, you gotta start watching what you're doing, or you're gonna be banged up for the girlfriend cruise to Norway" that Zelda and I had been planning for later in the month. I crawled back to bed, started back on my trusty pain twins, hobbled, groaned, and continued as best I could.

Ten days later at the Dallas Fort Worth airport (DFW), as I reached the top of the escalator taking me up to my flight to meet Zelda in New York for our cruise, my roller bag's front wheels

My Story

caught on the landing strip, throwing the bag on me and knocking me backward—yet again on my head and right side. Embarrassed, stunned, and unable to get off the ever-rising steps that kept coming up under and pushing me back down, it seemed surreal. I called out. Two young men pulled me up, gathered my things, and flagged down help ("Thank you, God!").

I hurt. My body screamed as the old-yet-unhealed injuries from the earlier falls rushed back to life and new ones set in. By the time I was released from the ER later that evening, I knew my trip wasn't going to happen. "Oh God!" My body, mind, and spirit were broken and bruised.

While in the ER, I'd swayed between beseeching God for help and pouring out prayers of gratitude. I'd come an inch away from being crippled or dead. My head could have been so injured I wouldn't have recovered. More bones could have broken in the fall. "Thank you, Jesus!" I was alive and reasonably lucid.

At first, still in shock, I was devastated because I couldn't go on my trip—all that planning, all that scenery and night skies I would miss. Mostly I would miss being with my bestie for two glorious weeks of laughing, sometimes crying, and always receiving the blessing beyond measure that comes from our thirty-five years of sisterhood. Hurt upon hurt, I sobbed.

Little did I realize in those early hours that the pain of missing the cruise would recede into my memories of other disappointments I'd had, and I'd be left with the reality that I also would miss everything for who knew how long—classes I was scheduled to teach and take, plans Bud and I had, events I'd help plan, luncheons and club meetings. Then, it dawned on me that I wouldn't be able to work on this book. My right shoulder, arm, and wrist were so damaged I couldn't use a keyboard. My back and ribs hurt too much to sit up for much more than a half hour. My brain was like Swiss cheese when it came to holding a thought. Putting two or three cohesive thoughts together and writing them down wasn't going to happen.

"Oh, God," I cried. My body ached, and my spirit was low.

Rarely given to self-pity and not being able to see a silver lining in the future was new to me. It was the first time I'd experienced an extended period of what Saint John of the Cross called the "dark night of the soul."

"Why, my soul, are you downcast? Why so disturbed within me?" (Ps 42:11 NRSVue).

The deep despair and depression troubled me more than the physical pain. I've suffered pain and disappointment many times. I couldn't bear the children I'd always wanted. This still hurts me to the bone when I let myself think of it. Both of my parents died painful deaths. You cannot go through such spiritual pain without being scarred for life. I'd experienced painful separations with people I loved. I'd fought two bouts of breast cancer. So why one night did I sink so low as to consider that maybe God didn't want me anymore and had left me incapable of doing anything?

That God had led me to earn an MA in Theology, write books on women's spirituality, keep a calendar chocked with speaking engagements and retreats, and accept the position of spiritual growth coordinator for a United Methodist women's group that spans most of Texas should have reassured me that God hadn't abandoned me. But I couldn't shake the darkness and fear.

In the deepest part of my soul, I knew that God loved me from the beginning, and no matter what I had done or do, God was, is, and always will be with me until the end of my life and beyond. And I knew the meaning of "the dark night of the soul." Yet, I was angry, hurt, and puzzled as to why I'd been rendered so useless that I felt maybe God didn't love me. In the deep crevasses of my soul, I never blamed God, but it was hard to see the situation clearly.

By this point I was praying the psalms constantly just to get a grip.

Two thoughts haunted my sleepless, aching nights. Does God want me to give up my career in writing and speaking? After all, I'm far past the age we think of as our productive years. And, if so, God, what will I do?

My Story

When Bud and I retired and moved to Fort Worth, a city we felt drawn to but knew no one, every day I prayed, "God, as I retire and make this move, please bless me with a loving church and friends, and now that I have time, use my talents to your service." I wondered, "Did I miss something in how things were turning out? If so, God, will you tell me what?"

For years I had Ps 139:13–16 taped to my mirror, where I could read it daily as I dressed:

> You are the one who created my innermost parts;
> you knit me together while I was still in my mother's womb.
> I give thanks to you that I was marvelously set apart.
> Your works are wonderful—I know that very well.
> My bones weren't hidden from you
> when I was being put together in a secret place,
> when I was being woven together in the deep parts of the earth.
> Your eyes saw my embryo,
> and on your scroll every day was written that was being formed for me,
> before any one of them had yet happened. (Ps 139:13–16 MSG)

So, what was God telling me through the falls? I thought I'd been living this psalm up to now. God had answered my prayer for a church, friends, and to use me. Was God now trying to tell me something about my future journey that I just wasn't getting?

Beyond my initial anger, I'd moved on to searching for answers while leaning into knowing that "no test or temptation that comes your way is beyond the course of what others have had to face. All you need to remember is that God will never let you down; he'll never let you be pushed past your limit; he'll always be there to help you come through it" (1 Cor 10:13 MSG).

Thank you, Jesus!

Although there was pain and confutation, blessings abounded. "Thank you, Jesus," for my husband, friends, family, and Jackie the sock thief who rarely left my side. My friend Linda brought me a basket of Easter flowers and a stuffed bunny. As I write I see it sitting in my office bookcase, still feeling the joy it brought (brings). Bunnies cure. Another friend, Debbie, brought a centerpiece from a UMW (United Methodist Women) circle meeting I'd missed. These are among many other kindnesses. I was flooded with cards, flowers, texts, calls, and *food*. Amy, my cousin in South Carolina, sent so much fruit via Sprouts that I had to share it with my housekeeper and neighbors to keep it from rotting before we could eat it. Although Bud cooks well, like all of us, he gets tired of it. The food blessed both of us. One card contained a Lucite angel that sits beside the bunny. Thank you, Lynn. Bestie Zelda was there for me every step of the way. Seeing her face during our weekly Zoom chats lifted my spirits like no others. I was over the moon when she and her family came to our house to view the total eclipse in early April. There were too many other friends who supported me to mention. Hell for me would be spending eternity without my girlfriends. "Thank you, God," for answering my prayer for friends.

During the days when the headache would subside, I read a couple of novels, a luxury I rarely allow myself to spend time on. "Thank you, Jesus," that new books had just come out by two of my favorite writers, Kristen Hannah (*The Women*) and Anna Quindlen (*After Annie*). But mostly I read books by well-known women Christian writers. They gave me hope and made me think about how God works in our lives for the good of the entire kindom: Anne Lamott, Kathleen Norris, Brené Brown, Savanah Guthrie, Rachael Held Evans, Barbara Brown Taylor, and others. These were sisters who'd faced dark nights and prevailed by the grace of God.

Shannon Martin's book, *The Ministry of Ordinary Place*, blew my socks off:

> I thought I had thrown my back out before, but now I know the other times were only drills. Now, I scoff at the younger me with her thrown-out back. I shrieked, clutching my lower spine, and somehow hobbled to my bed, where I tried to laugh it off with the kids in a shaky attempt at delusion. I told myself if I just lay flat for a few minutes with Siley's Minions ice pack, I would be fine. I would still make it to Bible study with my pan of brownies. Short story long, I was not okay. I did not make it to Bible study that night, nor did I make it anywhere other

My Story

than to the edge of despair for the next four days. I could not sit. I couldn't get comfortable in bed. Cory practically had to carry me to the bathroom, and I usually cried on the return voyage. Hand to heart, I worried I had fractured my spine. I thought the pivot might have triggered a spontaneous, undiscovered form of cancer, and it was already metastasizing. Haunted by the thought of a novel I'd read years ago about a young girl whose mother was in an iron lung for her entire childhood, I imagined my kids feeding me orange slices two or ten years into the future, showing me grainy pictures of all the events I had missed. Late into the night I moaned, "I don't know what to do," only interspersing it with the occasional, blanket apology, "I'm sorry." I'm not even sure who I was saying it to.[17]

With healing came the realization that God hadn't used the falls to stop me. By the end of 2023 I'd exhausted my body, mind, and spirit. I was running from project to project, meeting to meeting, and speaking engagement to speaking engagement. Right after *Aging in Spirit* came out in mid-March, it reached number 31 in sales in women's spirituality on Amazon. I had signings and interviews to do. Thanksgiving to Christmas, I was my usual busy self, plus putting the final touches on the proposal for this book so it could be published in 2024. My chronic fatigue syndrome and fibromyalgia were out of control. Yet, changing this pattern had never entered my mind, even as I'd dragged myself around from one task to the next—often into the night.

So entrenched I was in my fast-lane pace it took two more falls after my first tumble to get my attention. For over a year, my doctors, husband, and those who knew me best had been telling me to slow down because of stress. It's a wonder I didn't have a stroke or heart attack. Throughout it all, my friend Suzi, especially, kept begging me to slow down, that something was going to happen. Well, it did, and at first I couldn't even get myself to the bathroom!

After way too long of praying for answers, looking into empty space, and being scared, I realized that I'd missed the point God

---

17. Martin, *Ministry of Ordinary Places*, 91–92.

had been trying to make all along: "PhD, professor, theologian, speaker, writer, blogger, coordinator of women's soul care events, conference attendee, committee member, and organization officer for spiritual growth, *Heal thyself!*" Not, "*Stop.*"

I wanted to crawl in a hole. If laughing wouldn't have hurt so bad, I might have laughed out loud as I tried to make myself invisible for what I'd done to myself. Here I was: for weeks, well-credentialed me had been lamenting but not bothering to listen to how God was trying to respond. I'd failed Spirituality 101.

Finally, I was able to ask and address the question posed in *The Lives We Actually Have* by Kate Bowler and Jessica Richie:[18] "God, what is your call on my life? I am listening."

I began to thank and praise God through the psalms more fervently. First, I was grateful to God that I hadn't been killed or permanently maimed. Second, because the accidents stopped me in my tracks, I was forced to take a hard look at what I had done to my body, mind, and God-given spirit. I'd further decreased my already-limited energy. I'd sometimes put my marriage on hold (bless Bud, who'd stood by me despite rarely even having a meal together that hadn't been rushed). And I'd neglected friendships and the other people whom I love and love me. Yes, indeed, the falls and long healing process had given me the opportunity to see that I'd been sacrificing everything that means the most to me.

> The LORD is near to all who call upon him,
> to all who call upon him in truth.
> He fulfills the desire of those who fear him;
> he hears their cry and saves them.
> The LORD watches over all who love him. (Ps 145:18–20a NABRE)

Today, seven months later, I still have some pain where the rib was broken and the shoulder that sustained the contusions. I might never heal fully. Time will tell. I don't walk as well as I once did and never without some pain, and I'm slow. I can write only for so long without back pain. But thank you, Jesus, I'm up and ready

---

18. Bowler and Richie, *Lives We Actually Have*, loc. 460.

My Story

to go back to the things God has set before me, albeit fewer of them and at a manageable pace. Last night I turned down the opportunity to go on to the board of a nonprofit that caters to needy women and children. Yay me! I'm not the only one who can fill the spot and do it well. Today I made plans to visit Zelda in New Jersey in October—my first flight since the fall at DFW. Finally, I am able to write again.

> I have placed the Lord always in front of me. Because He is at my right hand, I will not be moved. And so my heart is glad. My soul is full of joy. My body also will rest without fear. For You will not give me over to the grave. And You will not allow Your Holy One to return to dust. You will show me the way of life. Being with You is to be full of joy. In Your right hand there is happiness forever. (Ps 16:8–11 NLV)

Join me now as we explore living the psalms. I pray my compressed journey of living the psalms of praise, trust, thanksgiving, lament, wisdom, and kinship will help you see how and where they can fit into your life and assist you in bringing God into your everyday world to a greater extent.

As you read each psalm, try to put yourself in the mind of the psalmist. What might have triggered the need to write it? To the extent that we know, I'll give you the history of each. But even if we don't know much about its history, you can imagine what might have been the cause. Then, imagine how and when you might use the song. Finally, go back to the verses that "grab" you and reread and contemplate them. Ask yourself why this verse or verses caught your attention. Is it trying to tell you something?

Ask the Holy Spirit to help you. "The Spirit helps us in our weakness, for we do not know how to pray [praise] as we ought, but that very Spirit intercedes with groanings too deep for words. And God, who searches hearts, knows what the mind of the Spirit is, because the Spirit intercedes for the saints according to the will of God" (Rom 8:26–27 NRSV).

This simple exercise will help you on your way to leaning on the words when needed.

PART I

Praise: Worship, Adoration, Acclamation, and Tribute

All that exists comes from him; all is by him and for him.
To him be the glory forever! Amen. (Rom 11:36 NJB)

From time immemorial, people have praised their gods. We're hardwired that way—to reach out and glorify God, the mystical root of our being. Our deepest heart of heart yearns to both praise God and exalt God's relationship with us.

In *Beyond the Enneagram*, Marilyn Vancil fleshes out this predisposition: "Beneath the many layers of our story is an even deeper story. All of us, consciously or unconsciously, long to be connected to the Source of life, where we can know true fulfillment, unconditional love, and peace. Whether we acknowledge it or not, our souls cry out for healing and wholeness with both subtle and loud expressions. The Psalmist echoes our deepest yearnings: 'O God, you are my God; I earnestly search for you. My soul thirsts for you; my whole body longs for you in this parched and weary land where there is no water.'"[1]

To no surprise, praise and adoration are woven through every psalm, irrespective of its primary purpose, just as they do when we

---

1. Vancil, *Beyond the Enneagram*, 27.

pray, sing, and meditate. Even saying "Oh, God" or "Thank you, Jesus" implies praise and acclamation of God's greatness. Think about this a minute. Isn't this what we mean when uttering the phrases? Writing this gives me chills. "Thank you, Jesus."

Three major themes run through psalms of praise.

God is great. As a kid, I loved the folk song about Johnny Appleseed, the real-life John Chapman, who traveled through the Midwest planting apple trees in the early 1800s. "The lord is good to me, and so I thank the Lord." It still makes me happy simply because it does. If that isn't praise, I don't know what would be. I imagine that's how the psalmist felt when creating praise songs to God.

Praising God helps us, and of course, pleases God (Heb 12:28), just as we appreciate those who affirm and love us. However, it is we, not God, who truly benefit from worshiping our creator and sustainer, our "help in ages past" (Ps 90), and the one whom we trust. For when we praise God, we recall all that God has been, is, and will be to us throughout our lives.

When we praise God, it also helps others. We don't stand alone in God. We're part of God's people. Thus, when we praise God, we strengthen our godly ties both to God and to each other.

CHAPTER 1

Psalm 145

PSALM 145, ATTRIBUTED TO David, declares the goodness of God. It confronts our egocentrism with the truth that we were created to live in and for something vastly bigger than ourselves. I found myself in this situation not long ago and had to have a conversation with myself about trying to force my way regarding a women's class I was working on with others. I became Jen in Kayla's story. "Duh!" I finally realized this was no way act, which brings us to the second purpose of Ps 145. Here, David praises God for caring for everyone, not just for him.

The psalm reminds me one of my favorite Taizé chants, "Bless the Lord, My Soul."[1] I love it so much that I'm listening to it while writing this chapter.

PSALM 145

I will exalt you, my God the King;
I will praise your name for ever and ever.
Every day I will praise you
and extol your name for ever and ever.

---

1. Berthier, "Bless the Lord, My Soul."

Great is the Lord and most worthy of praise;
his greatness no one can fathom.
One generation commends your works to another;
they tell of your mighty acts.
They speak of the glorious splendor of your majesty—
and I will meditate on your wonderful works.
They tell of the power of your awesome works—
and I will proclaim your great deeds.
They celebrate your abundant goodness
and joyfully sing of your righteousness.

The Lord is gracious and compassionate,
slow to anger and rich in love.

The Lord is good to all;
he has compassion on all he has made.
All your works praise you, Lord;
your faithful people extol you.
They tell of the glory of your kingdom
and speak of your might,
so that all people may know of your mighty acts
and the glorious splendor of your kingdom.
Your kingdom is an everlasting kingdom,
and your dominion endures through all generations.

The Lord is trustworthy in all he promises
and faithful in all he does.
The Lord upholds all who fall
and lifts up all who are bowed down.
The eyes of all look to you,
and you give them their food at the proper time.
You open your hand
and satisfy the desires of every living thing.

The Lord is righteous in all his ways
and faithful in all he does.
The Lord is near to all who call on him,
to all who call on him in truth.
He fulfills the desires of those who fear him;
he hears their cry and saves them.
The Lord watches over all who love him,

Psalm 145

but all the wicked he will destroy.

My mouth will speak in praise of the LORD.
Let every creature praise his holy name
for ever and ever. (Ps 145 NIV)

In Daphne Simpkins' book *Kingdom Come*, one of the characters quotes Ps 145:14–16: "The Lord upholds all who fall, and raises up all those who are bowed down. The eyes of all look expectantly to You, and You give them their food in due season. You open Your hand and satisfy the desire of every living thing."[2]

This is a reminder that a psalm doesn't have to be used in full to make a point. The words aren't Scripture that must be read from top to bottom and sometimes in the context of an entire chapter to get their meaning. When you need a quick punch-up from the Holy Spirit, feel free to use sections of your favorite psalms.

---

2. Simpkins, *Kingdom Come*, 197.

CHAPTER 2

Psalm 146

IN THE OLD JEWISH tradition, Ps 146 was penned by David. It's a beautiful tribute to God's gifts of healing, restoration, protection, and wholeness throughout our lives and a go-to Scripture to read when we're afraid, insecure, or doubting ourselves. As with other psalms of praise, it lauds God for caring for others with the same need and ends exalting God for being here through eternity for everyone.

PSALM 146

>Praise the LORD!
>Praise the LORD, O my soul!
>I will praise the LORD as long as I live;
>I will sing praises to my God while I have my being.
>
>Put not your trust in princes,
>in a son of man, in whom there is no salvation.
>When his breath departs, he returns to the earth;
>on that very day his plans perish.
>
>Blessed is he whose help is the God of Jacob,
>whose hope is in the LORD his God,
>who made heaven and earth,
>the sea, and all that is in them,

Psalm 146

who keeps faith forever;
who executes justice for the oppressed,
who gives food to the hungry.

The LORD sets the prisoners free;
the LORD opens the eyes of the blind.
The LORD lifts up those who are bowed down;
the LORD loves the righteous.
The LORD watches over the sojourners;
he upholds the widow and the fatherless,
but the way of the wicked he brings to ruin.

The LORD will reign forever,
your God, O Zion, to all generations.
Praise the LORD! (Ps 146 ESV)

CHAPTER 3

Psalm 63

THERE'S LITTLE DOUBT AMONG historians that Ps 63 was written by David while fleeing Saul's army and living in the wilderness of Judah. You must see the area to realize fully how desperate his situation was. With little water and nothing but rocky earth, barren hills, and scrub bushes for miles, little was available to protect him from the elements and wild beasts. Caves in the area are simply rock crevasses. From these bare defenses he praised God for comfort and protection. He leaned on God's grace and assurance that his trials would pass—that he would be OK.

Sarah Bessy writes, "When we have suffered, when we have been bruised and scarred, when our light has been blown out, when we are ground beneath someone else's heel, I hope to remember we belong to a God who is faithful to restore us. We aren't invisible to Jesus or embarrassing to Jesus, nor are we unwelcome."[1]

PSALM 63

> O God, you are my God,
> and I long for you.
> My whole being desires you;
> like a dry, worn-out, and waterless land,

---

1. Bessy, *Miracles*, 140.

Psalm 63

my soul is thirsty for you.
Let me see you in the sanctuary;
let me see how mighty and glorious you are.
Your constant love is better than life itself,
and so I will praise you.
I will give you thanks as long as I live;
I will raise my hands to you in prayer.
My soul will feast and be satisfied,
and I will sing glad songs of praise to you.

As I lie in bed, I remember you;
all night long I think of you,
because you have always been my help.
In the shadow of your wings I sing for joy.
I cling to you,
and your hand keeps me safe.

Those who are trying to kill me
will go down into the world of the dead.
They will be killed in battle,
and their bodies eaten by wolves.
Because God gives him victory,
the king will rejoice.
Those who make promises in God's name will praise him,
but the mouths of liars will be shut. (Ps 63 GNT)

CHAPTER 4

Psalm 40

LIKE PS 63, Ps 40 may have been written during one of David's exiles or his early reign as the young, beleaguered king. Either way, he felt as though he was hopelessly stuck in a slimy pit that he couldn't climb out of without God's help. This is a great metaphor for when we're in a seemingly no-win situation of being damned if we do or damned if we don't. Excruciating!

One of the best examples I know was when a coworker's twenty-two-year-old son became hooked on just about every drug known to humankind. Night after night she questioned whether she should take a hard line and possibly throw him into a life of drugs or whether she should try to work with him at home with the possibility of him wrecking their household and his siblings' lives. With God's help and the fortitude of David facing Goliath, she took a middle road. It's a long story, but at the end of three years—thank you, Jesus—she was able to get him off drugs, rehabilitated, and into college. Today, he's an EMT helping others who need triage, many from overdoses. While not all stories end so happily, hers is a good example of sticking with God when the worst happens.

PSALM 40

I waited patiently for the Lord,
and He turned to me, and heard my cry.
He also brought me up out of a horrible pit,
out of the miry clay,
and set my feet on a rock,
and established my steps.
He has put a new song in my mouth,
even praise to our God;
many will see it, and fear,
and will trust in the Lord.
Blessed is the man
who places trust in the Lord,
but does not turn toward the proud,
nor those falling away to falsehood.
O Lord my God,
You have done many wonderful works,
and Your thoughts toward us
cannot be compared;
if I would declare and speak of them,
they are more than can be numbered.
Sacrifice and offering You did not desire;
You have opened up my ears to listen.
Burnt offering and sin offering
You have not required.
Then I said, "Behold, I have come;
in the scroll of the book it is written of me,
I delight to do Your will, O my God;
Your law is within my inward parts."
I have proclaimed righteousness in the great congregation;
I have not held back my lips,
O Lord, You know.
I have not hidden Your righteousness within my heart;
I have declared Your faithfulness and Your salvation;
I have not concealed Your lovingkindness and Your truth
from the great congregation.
Do not withhold Your compassion from me, O Lord;
may Your lovingkindness and Your truth always guard me.
For innumerable evils have surrounded me;

my iniquities have overtaken me, so that I am not able
to look up;
they are more than the hairs of my head
so that my heart fails me.
Be pleased, O Lord, to deliver me;
O Lord, make haste to help me.
May those seeking to snatch away my life
be ashamed and confounded together;
may those who desire my harm
be driven backward and dishonored.
May those who say to me "Aha, aha!"
be appalled on account of their shame.
May all those who seek You
rejoice and be glad in You;
may those who love Your salvation say continually,
"The Lord is magnified."
But I am poor and needy;
yet the Lord thinks about me.
You are my help and my deliverer;
do not delay, O my God. (Ps 40 MEV)

CHAPTER 5

Psalm 8

PSALM 8 IS A meditation on and admiration of the glory and greatness of God. It begins and ends with the same acknowledgment of God's majesty. As proof, the psalmist gives instances of God's goodness and grace to us small beings in this vast universe.

"One snowy morning recently, I felt at loose ends, disconnected from myself, from God," Shauna Niequest wrote in *Present Over Perfect*.

> I'd been sick, and my mind had been anxious. I practiced lectio divina [slow reading and retreading of Scripture] selecting a passage from Psalm 8: "When I look at your heavens, the work of your fingers, the moon and the stars, which you have set in place, what is man that you are mindful of him, and the son of man that you care for him?" As those words began to take root in me, as I read and reread them, as I prayed and listened, I felt my tangled spirit begin to untangle. I felt my breath slow and deepen. I felt a part of the natural world, governed by a good God, created with care and attentiveness. I felt my daughter-ness, my place in the family of God. And I exhaled.[1]

Sometimes we just need to step out of ourselves and let God untangle our souls, realizing that God is in control of all creation.

---

1. Niequest, *Present Over Perfect*, 86.

PSALM 8

O Eternal, our Lord,
Your majestic name is heard throughout the earth;
Your magnificent glory shines far above the skies.
From the mouths *and souls* of infants and toddlers, *the most innocent,*
You have decreed power to stop Your adversaries
and quash those who seek revenge.

When I gaze to the skies and meditate on Your creation—
on the moon, stars, *and all* You have made,
I can't help but wonder why You care about mortals—
sons *and daughters* of men—
specks of dust floating about the cosmos.

But You placed the son of man just beneath God
and honored him like royalty, crowning him with glory and honor.
You ordained him to govern the works of Your hands,
to nurture the offspring of Your divine imagination;
You placed everything *on earth* beneath his feet:
All kinds of domesticated animals,
even the wild animals in the fields *and forests,*
The birds of the sky and the fish of the sea,
all *the multitudes of living things* that travel the currents of the oceans.

O Eternal, our Lord,
Your majestic name is heard throughout the earth. (Ps 8 VOICE)

CHAPTER 6

Psalm 89

PSALM 89 WAS WRITTEN during a stressful time in the history of the Jewish people. Jerusalem was in ruins after David's reign. Without a godly king, the people had lost control over their destiny. In this weak and helpless condition, they felt God was angry with them. Then, in the darkness of this hopelessness, they remembered the greatness of God's promises to David. It gave them the hope they needed to survive their present conditions along with the promise of delivery. Seems I've heard this story somewhere else.

Does this ring a bell with anything going on in our world today? Last night Zelda and I watched the magnificent Yom Kippur service from the Central Synagogue in New York City, where the pain of the war started last year on October 7 floated like a dark specter. The same specter also floats in Gaza, Ukraine, Sudan, Yemeni, and too many other places to mention. As I write a month before our presidential election, the specter of chaos, hate, and possible disruption hangs heavy in the United States. All of creation needs God, who "rules the raging of the sea; when its waves rise, you still them" (Ps 89:9 NRSV).

So too do we, in our individual lives, need God to still the water when it rages. Psalm 89 fit my condition like a glove after my falls. And it's your psalm when the water rises in your life and the cold wind howls. Substitute in whatever condition you're in and replace the promises God made to David with the promises of God's care, concern, love, and grace brought to us by Jesus.

PSALM 89

I will sing of your steadfast love, O LORD, for ever;
with my mouth I will proclaim your faithfulness to all
   generations.
I declare that your steadfast love is established for ever;
your faithfulness is as firm as the heavens.

You said, 'I have made a covenant with my chosen one,
I have sworn to my servant David:
"I will establish your descendants for ever,
and build your throne for all generations."' *Selah*

Let the heavens praise your wonders, O LORD,
your faithfulness in the assembly of the holy ones.
For who in the skies can be compared to the LORD?
Who among the heavenly beings is like the LORD,
a God feared in the council of the holy ones,
great and awesome above all that are around him?
O LORD God of hosts,
who is as mighty as you, O LORD?
Your faithfulness surrounds you.
You rule the raging of the sea;
when its waves rise, you still them.
You crushed Rahab like a carcass;
you scattered your enemies with your mighty arm.
The heavens are yours, the earth also is yours;
the world and all that is in it—you have founded them.
The north and the south—you created them;
Tabor and Hermon joyously praise your name.
You have a mighty arm;
strong is your hand, high your right hand.
Righteousness and justice are the foundation of your throne;
steadfast love and faithfulness go before you.
Happy are the people who know the festal shout,
who walk, O LORD, in the light of your countenance;
they exult in your name all day long,

Psalm 89

and extol your righteousness.
For you are the glory of their strength;
by your favour our horn is exalted.
For our shield belongs to the LORD,
our king to the Holy One of Israel.

Then you spoke in a vision to your faithful one, and said:
'I have set the crown on one who is mighty,

I have exalted one chosen from the people.
I have found my servant David;
with my holy oil I have anointed him;
my hand shall always remain with him;
my arm also shall strengthen him.
The enemy shall not outwit him,
the wicked shall not humble him.
I will crush his foes before him
and strike down those who hate him.
My faithfulness and steadfast love shall be with him;
and in my name his horn shall be exalted.
I will set his hand on the sea
and his right hand on the rivers.
He shall cry to me, "You are my Father,
my God, and the Rock of my salvation!"
I will make him the firstborn,
the highest of the kings of the earth.
For-ever I will keep my steadfast love for him,
and my covenant with him will stand firm.
I will establish his line for ever,
and his throne as long as the heavens endure.
If his children forsake my law
and do not walk according to my ordinances,
if they violate my statutes
and do not keep my commandments,
then I will punish their transgression with the rod
and their iniquity with scourges;
but I will not remove from him my steadfast love,
or be false to my faithfulness.
I will not violate my covenant,
or alter the word that went forth from my lips
Once and for all I have sworn by my holiness;

I will not lie to David.
His line shall continue for ever,
and his throne endure before me like the sun.
It shall be established for ever like the moon,
an enduring witness in the skies.' *Selah*

But now you have spurned and rejected him;
you are full of wrath against your anointed.
You have renounced the covenant with your servant;
you have defiled his crown in the dust.
You have broken through all his walls;
you have laid his strongholds in ruins.
All who pass by plunder him;
he has become the scorn of his neighbours.
You have exalted the right hand of his foes;
you have made all his enemies rejoice.
Moreover, you have turned back the edge of his sword,
and you have not supported him in battle.
You have removed the sceptre from his hand,
and hurled his throne to the ground.
You have cut short the days of his youth;
you have covered him with shame. *Selah*

How long, O LORD? Will you hide yourself for ever?
How long will your wrath burn like fire?
Remember how short my time is—
for what vanity you have created all mortals!
Who can live and never see death?
Who can escape the power of Sheol? *Selah*

LORD, where is your steadfast love of old,
which by your faithfulness you swore to David?
Remember, O LORD, how your servant is taunted;
how I bear in my bosom the insults of the peoples,
with which your enemies taunt, O LORD,
with which they taunted the footsteps of your anointed.

Blessed be the LORD for ever.
Amen and Amen. (Ps 89 NRSVA)

CHAPTER 7

Psalm 121

"I will lift up my eyes to the hills. From where does my help come?" Psalm 121 was written to instill confidence in God's grace to keep Hebrew pilgrims safe as they journeyed up Mount Zion to Jerusalem to worship. These words flooded my mind as the magnificent view of Jerusalem, sitting on the hill, came closer when Bud and I drove toward the city at sundown. What a spiritual lift it must have given the early Hebrews as they drew nearer to their destination, some of them having walked for days, if not weeks.

Centuries later, Psalm 121 remains a go-to favorite for we who journey and reach out to God for assistance and assurance. The journey can be anything from not knowing how our husband is and will be while following the ambulance taking him to the emergency room to knowing you're about to give a speech to an unknown group. Maybe it's writing a book! Overall, it's the ultimate journey we are taking to God, climbing, stumbling, reaching a beautiful plateau, or of simply needing to take a break when things get tough.

PSALM 121

I lift up my eyes to the hills.
From whence does my help come?

My help comes from the LORD,
who made heaven and earth.

He will not let your foot be moved,
he who keeps you will not slumber.
Behold, he who keeps Israel
will neither slumber nor sleep.

The LORD is your keeper;
the LORD is your shade
on your right hand.
The sun shall not smite you by day,
nor the moon by night.

The LORD will keep you from all evil;
he will keep your life.
The LORD will keep
your going out and your coming in
from this time forth and for evermore. (Ps 121 RSV)

The following is a personalized version of this psalm by author Nan C. Merrill in *Psalms for Praying*:

My heart's eyes behold you
Divine Glory!
From whence does my help come?
My help comes from You,
who created heaven and earth.
You strengthen and uphold me,
You who are ever by my side.
Behold You who watch over the
nations.
will see all hearts Awaken
to the light.
For you are the Great Counselor:
You dwell within all our hearts,
that we might respond to the
Universal Heart—
Like the sun, that nourishes us by day
like the stars that guide the
wayfarer at night.
In You we shall not be afraid of

PSALM 121

the darkness, for
You are the Light of our life.
May You keep us in our going out
and our coming in
from this time forth and
forever more.[1]

---

1. Merrill, *Psalms for Praying*, 257.

PART II

Assurance: Trust, Safety, Help, and Confidence in God

For I am convinced that neither death, nor life, nor angels, nor rulers, nor things present, nor things to come, nor powers, nor height, nor depth, nor anything else in all creation will be able to separate us from the love of God in Christ Jesus our Lord. (Rom 8:38–39 NRSVue)

NO MATTER HOW LONG we live, we'll never feel we get sufficient confirmation that God loves us and has our backs. Even the greatest saints and folks we think have it all together spiritually quest for greater love and assurance. We know from Scripture that until the end of their lives, God's people craved the assurance, trust, safety, help, and confidence no matter how much God had assured them in the past. For us, this can mean this morning. Maybe it's now. This isn't so different between God and us and between someone we love and us. When Danny, my grandchild, was a toddler and we were out somewhere, they sometimes waddled ahead of me. Yet, with every few steps, they'd look back to make sure I was there. Reassured that Grandma Karen was just behind, they'd go on until the next need for assurance.

When I need confirmation from God, my first thought is *love*. For, like Paul, I'm certain that nothing can separate me from the love of God. In that, I'm certain I can depend on God, who loves me, to care for me, no matter what. Just writing this warms my soul.

Similarly, Fr. Richard Rohr believes, "We are already in union with God! There is an absolute, eternal union between God and the soul of everything. At the deepest level, we are 'hidden with Christ in God' (Col 3:3) and 'the whole creation . . . is being brought into the same glorious freedom as the children of God' (Rom 8:21)."[1]

In 1878, Fanny J. Crosby, the blind lyricist of somewhere between five thousand and nine thousand hymns (many of which are still are sung today), penned the mighty words, "Blessed assurance, Jesus is mine."[2] One hundred fifty years later, isn't this what we still want? Isn't that what the psalmists wanted?

Unfortunately, today, as Alissa Quart writes in *Bootstrapped*, "We live in a nation that demands we be impossibly self-reliant."[3] When I was a grad student, I pinned a poster on my bedroom wall telling me daily that "if it's meant to be, it's up to me." Because this notion is reinforced everywhere we turn and from all sides, it's no wonder women push themselves to be strivers, high achievers, control freaks, and perfectionists. I count myself among them.

So too, we are a society that has lost our trust in our government. 9/11 broke our confidence that we are safe. On a personal level, by the time we reach our teens/early adulthood, likely, we've lost trust in our decision-making abilities, relationships, career(s), bodies, financial situation(s), love, and on and on. As we age, these issues accumulate with every year, and more will join them in the future. When we hit middle age, it seems to start all over. No wonder those who never find hope become embittered, spiteful, hateful, and distrustful of themselves and others. For the same reason (feeling lost, worthless, etc.), the notion of hope runs like a river through the Bible. Think about all the hymns you know that speak

---

1. Rohr, "Prophetic Path."
2. Crosby, "Blessed Assurance."
3. Quart, *Bootstrapped*, x.

Psalm 121

to this need. As I write, I can think of at least a half dozen off the top of my head.

Unless they've been traumatized and before society teaches them otherwise, kids who've been taught to pray don't think this way. When they say nightly prayers, they're confident and approach God full on with their requests and concerns.

In *The Particular Sadness of Lemon Cake*, Aimee Bender writes about nine-year-old Rose saying her prayers: "That night, as I burrowed into the sheets, my mother still tucking in sheets better than anyone, I closed my eyes and went through my usual routine, which involved thanking God . . . for the vending machine at school, for the sad lady with the hairnet who still worked at the cafeteria, for the existence of [my friend] George, and for whoever ate my mother's cookies at the co-op."[4]

My mother tells the story that just before Thanksgiving when I was three, I asked God to keep all the gobblers from getting killed. She had no idea where this came from, as she'd never mentioned how the roasted turkey would come to be on our table. Although I have no memory of the prayer, what I am certain of is that I knew God was hearing me and would take care of some turkeys.

I wish that when I took the falls I could/would have approached God with the same assurance I'd had then. Instead, I simply couldn't give myself over to it fully. That's where reading and rereading the psalms came in. Each time I went to back to them, they helped build my assurance that God was holding my hand and taking care of my future, even if I couldn't see it.

Ignatian spirituality tells us that when we name our desires, we trust that it is God who has placed them in our hearts. Thus, we can be confident that God will bring that desire to fruition. On our part, we've got to make sure our desires are in alignment with God's. Remember the woman who wanted God to kill her husband and his new wife? Clearly, she didn't get this second part.

In Part II, we'll discuss examples of the more well-known psalms of comfort and assurance other than the two most popular, Pss 91 and 23. I'm saving them for the conclusion. Since they are

---

4. Bender, *Sadness of Lemon Cake*, 112.

the epitome of God's universal message of hope, praise, gratitude, and understanding of kinship, like the old song says, I've saved the best for last. Nonetheless, the psalms in Part II are mighty in their ability to see us through whatever we face.

CHAPTER 8

Psalm 125

PSALM 125 WAS WRITTEN to be communal and shared like the litanies some denominations incorporate into their worship. It's the same when we come together with any group to seek God's assurance. Remember all the public gatherings after 9/11?

But don't discount communal psalms as being only for the good of a group when they are used in a formal setting. In *Grace Can Lead Us Home*, Kevin Nye wrote, "So much holy and transformative work happens in the innocuous moments when people are simply together, sharing an experience, participating in an activity, and being humans in community."[1]

Although the author of Ps 125 is unknown, it's believed to have been written after the Hebrews returned from the Babylonian exile (Neh 6:12–13) to find their land taken over by others. Many of the Jews who had not been taken in captivity had turned to idols. It's a song of assurance that God was on the side of those who'd remained faithful and would protect them from the evils of what they faced. We are hearing rumbles of this today in the United States, not just that our land is being overtaken, but many believe that our beliefs about God are. Similarly, the Middle East, as always, is in such turmoil over land and differences in beliefs today that our news sources are predicting an all-out war.

---

1. Nye, *Grace Can Lead Us Home*, 30.

When we make the psalm personal, we recreate the same atmosphere of knowing that God will help us overcome the slings and arrows we now have and will encounter throughout our lives.

PSALM 125

Those who trust in the Lord are like Mount Zion,
which cannot be moved but abides forever.
As the mountains surround Jerusalem,
so the Lord surrounds his people,
from this time on and forevermore.
For the scepter of wickedness shall not rest
on the land allotted to the righteous,
so that the righteous might not stretch out
their hands to do wrong.
Do good, O Lord, to those who are good,
and to those who are upright in their hearts.
But those who turn aside to their own crooked ways
the Lord will lead away with evildoers.
Peace be upon Israel! (Ps 125 NRSV)

CHAPTER 9

Psalm 16

UNLIKE PS 125, IT'S believed Ps 16 was written by David as a personal affirmation of his trust and security in God. This type of psalms is called a *miktam*, meaning "a golden nugget of wisdom." Pastor and noted speaker David Guzik writes, "It seems David wrote this psalm from a time of trouble, because he asked for preservation, knew that he would not be moved (Ps 16:8), and had confidence in some kind of resurrection (Ps 16:10). Yet the *tone* of this psalm is not despair or complaint; it is settled joy. Despite his trouble, David had a praising confidence in his God."[1]

I love the idea of settled joy. Think about it a minute. Do you ever feel God's joy? I sometimes am overcome with a calm, peaceful, deep joy that makes me want to sing the kid's song "I've Got the Joy, Joy, Joy Down in My Heart,"[2] which we belted out at Vacation Bible School. One of my groups chose the theme "I've Got the Joy" for a women's retreat early in 2023 and sang the song for our opening. Imagine eighty women standing and belting out about having God's joy so loud someone walking by would have thought it was a room of first graders. We drowned out the keyboard. We clapped. Most danced. You can't sit still and whisper this song!

---

1. Guzik, "Psalm 16" (emphasis original).
2. Cooke, "I've Got the Joy."

Not too long after that retreat, I read Angela Williams Gorrell's description of holding Bible classes in a women's prison: "This particular night, everyone was out of their seats, and we were jumping and dancing and singing 'This Little Light of Mine' so loudly that one of the corrections officers came into the room."[3] She watched what was happening with amazement. She joined us and started clapping her hands and smiling. Joy gathers. As we sang, our ashes (failures and disappointments) seemed to become crowns of beauty, our mourning turned to joy, and our spirits of despair transformed into praise. Our music became an act of resistance to all of the forms of death that had happened and were happening in our lives. Our singing turned into embodied opposition to our fear, anger, and profound loss. Our joyful noise opposed the imprisonment of bodies and minds, and suddenly, we were rejoicing in what ought to be. Our dancing, jumping, clapping, and singing together pushed against voices that declared "You are alone," "You are worthless," or "There is no hope."

Williams Gorrell goes on: "Joy has a wondrous way of seizing our attention. It often comes swiftly and powerfully. Joy can be a gift of the breaking in of goodness, beauty, and truth amid brokenness."[4] I think of this as God's healing joy.

Psalm 16 serves both as an affirmation of God's steadfastness in our lives and our steadfast faith in God, plus our joy in God's faithfulness. It certainly fits when we are in mental distress about our relationship with God, such as my dark night of the soul and the bright star of morning that comes when clouds roll away. As I've matured in my faith, Ps 16 has become one of my favorites. It sums up and praises my ever-deepening relationship with and love for God. I find refuge in God. With God's help I grow closer to my fellow Christians. Daily I rely more and more on God to direct my life and counsel me when I hurt or stray (as during my dark period after the falls). For these, along with the psalmist, I rejoice.

We're going to read the psalm in two versions, the more traditional NRSVue and *The Message*. This second one isn't an actual

---

3. Gorrell, *Gravity of Joy*, 118.
4. Gorrell, *Gravity of Joy*, 118.

PSALM 16

translation but a well-respected, rephrased version that addresses the issues of our day. This is because sometimes it's hard to relate to the strict biblical translations because they use phrases, terms, and metaphors that are foreign to our ways of understanding, much less how we live our daily lives. Have you ever wondered why so many movies are updated, recast, and remade for the current generation, or why an old rock song is recorded years later with an updated beat and maybe a few added lyrics? It's the same with psalms. To live them, we've got to understand them.

PSALM 16

> Protect me, O God, for in you I take refuge.
> I say to the Lord, "You are my Lord;
> I have no good apart from you."
>
> As for the holy ones in the land, they are the noble ones
> in whom is all my delight.
>
> Those who choose another god multiply their sorrows;
> their drink offerings of blood I will not pour out
> or take their names upon my lips.
>
> The Lord is my chosen portion and my cup;
> you hold my lot.
> The boundary lines have fallen for me in pleasant
>   places;
> I have a goodly heritage.
>
> I bless the Lord, who gives me counsel;
> in the night also my heart instructs me.
> I keep the Lord always before me;
> because he is at my right hand, I shall not be moved.
>
> Therefore my heart is glad, and my soul rejoices;
> my body also rests secure
> For you do not give me up to Sheol [place of the dead or
> "hollow," not hell]
> or let your faithful one see the Pit [a hole or place of woe].

You show me the path of life.
In your presence there is fullness of joy;
in your right hand are pleasures forevermore.
(Ps 16 NRSVue)

PSALM 16 FROM THE MESSAGE

Keep me safe, O God,
I've run for dear life to you.
I say to God, "Be my Lord!"
Without you, nothing makes sense.

And these God-chosen lives all around—
what splendid friends they make!

Don't just go shopping for a god.
Gods are not for sale.
I swear I'll never treat god-names
like brand-names.

My choice is you, God, first and only.
And now I find I'm *your* choice!
You set me up with a house and yard.
And then you made me your heir!

The wise counsel God gives when I'm awake
is confirmed by my sleeping heart.
Day and night I'll stick with God;
I've got a good thing going and I'm not letting go.

I'm happy from the inside out,
and from the outside in, I'm firmly formed.
You canceled my ticket to hell—
that's not my destination!

Now you've got my feet on the life path,
all radiant from the shining of your face.
Ever since you took my hand,
I'm on the right way. (Ps 16 MSG)

CHAPTER 10

Psalm 54

PSALM 54 IS A request for guidance, compassion and protection, another *maskil* attributed to David. It was written when he was being chased by King Saul. Today I think of it as a plea from strife and fear when we're surrounded by temptations, people who don't have our best interests at heart, and the complications from when life forces us to deal with problems that continuously plague us with no seeming offer of relief. What comes to mind are ongoing, specific problems in our family, being part of the sandwich generation, suffering systemic racism (sexism, ageism, bullying, ethnocentrism, ableism, sizeism, homophobia, and the other isms), long-term illnesses, marriage and family conflict, and long-term economic conditions. I'm sure you can add to the list.

When these seemingly endless problems get you down, turn to Ps 54, read the words slowly, and let them comfort you, even if momentarily. As always, think of the psalm as a metaphor, not literally.

PSALM 54

Save me, O God, by thy name,
and vindicate me by thy might.

Hear my prayer, O God;
give ear to the words of my mouth.

For insolent men have risen against me,
ruthless men seek my life;
they do not set God before them. *Selah*

Behold, God is my helper;
the Lord is the upholder of my life.
He will requite my enemies with evil;
in thy faithfulness put an end to them.

With a freewill offering I will sacrifice to thee;
I will give thanks to thy name, O LORD, for it is good.
For thou hast delivered me from every trouble,
and my eye has looked in triumph on my enemies.
(Ps 54 RSV)

CHAPTER 11

Psalm 62

PSALM 62 IS A tough one for a really tough time in David's life. His son, Absalom, had rebelled against David and was killed in battle. Earlier, Absolom had killed his half brother for raping their sister, Tamar. David's life and kingdom were crumbling before his very eyes.

Although most of our betrayals aren't of this mythic proportion, we've all been betrayed, and betrayals can be among the greatest hurts of all. In the least, such as Kayla's difficulty with the controlling committee member, they leave us feeling unprotected. At their most severe, they wreck our lives. The closer the one who betrays us, such as our spouse and other family members, the more painful.

Sometimes it's a group or group leader. Back in the early 2000s, I served on the board of an international Christian nonprofit foundation that built churches, orphanages, senior citizens' centers, and schools throughout Asia, but primarily in China. Part of my responsibility was to work with a film crew as the on-camera interviewer to document how women were an integral part of Chinese Christian organizations, including the woman who ranked at the top of the organization. Before starting, we got permission from the Chinese government. Because of my schedule we filmed during several summers so I could use vacation time. Just as we'd gotten our footage and our technician was editing and dubbing it back in our studio, we had a board meeting. During lunch, our CEO offhandedly mentioned that the Chinese government had shut down our project, laughed about how slippery it was to work with them, and blew it off. Evidently it wasn't important enough for him to have put it on the meeting agenda.

I lost my breath and was caught somewhere between chocking and sobbing. It wasn't that the government had pulled my project. They're known for such. What hurt to my soul was that no one had offered me the courtesy of telling me in private what had happened. And no one ever mentioned it again after the meeting. Months of work during boiling Chinese summers and traveling across the country with a crew and equipment were gone. Moreover, a project close to my heart for women disappeared into thin air. Because of cultural differences regarding rank and respect for Asian men in high places, I wasn't able to confront the CEO. If I'd ever been in a situation to lean into Ps 62, it was then.

For this psalm I'm quoting from the New Jerusalem Bible. I like it for its clarity, and updated words and phrases.

PSALM 62

In God alone there is rest for my soul, from him comes my safety;

with him alone for my rock, my safety, my fortress, I can never fall.

How many times will you come rushing at a man, all of you, to bring him down like a wall already leaning over, like a rampart undermined?

Deceit their sole intention, their delight is to mislead; with lies on their lips they bless aloud, while cursing inwardly. (pause)

Rest in God alone, my soul! He is the source of my hope;

Psalm 62

with him alone for my rock, my safety, my fortress, I can never fall;

rest in God, my safety, my glory, the rock of my strength. In God, I find shelter;

rely on him people, at all times; unburden your hearts to him, God is a shelter for us.

Ordinary men are only a puff of wind, important men[*a] delusion; put both in the scales and up they go, lighter than a puff of wind.

Put no reliance on extortion, no empty hopes in robbery; though riches may increase, keep your heart detached.

God has spoken once, twice I have heard this: it is for God to be strong, for you,

Lord, to be loving; and you yourself repay man as his works deserve. (Ps 62 NJB)

CHAPTER 12

Psalm 20

PSALM 20 IS THE perfect song of David for helping us to pray during times of uncertainties and confusion. David, through the inspiration of the Holy Spirit, sings a song of great assurance, protection, power, and rest for the person who rests in the Lord.

I think of it as a means of assurance and rescue during hurricanes, floods, and other natural disasters; violence in our communities; humanitarian crises; family distress; personal woes; and confusion over identity and purpose. These are but a few issues that face the average person today. In times such as these, you may feel too crippled to even pray for your own internal struggles, let alone the world in general.

Notice the word "let" in verses 2–5, indicating that God doesn't demand us to ask for help but offers the loving option of helping us.

PSALM 20

> I pray that the LORD answers you
> whenever you are in trouble.
> Let the name of Jacob's God protect you.
> Let God send help to you from the sanctuary
> and support you from Zion.

Psalm 20

Let God recall your many grain offerings;
let him savor your entirely burned offerings. *Selah*
Let God grant what is in your heart
and fulfill all your plans.
Then we will rejoice that you've been helped.
We will fly our flags in the name of our God.
Let the Lord fulfill all your requests!

Now I know that the Lord saves his anointed one;
God answers his anointed one
from his heavenly sanctuary,
answering with mighty acts of salvation
achieved by his strong hand.
Some people trust in chariots, others in horses;
but we praise the Lord's name.
They will collapse and fall,
but we will stand up straight and strong.

Lord, save the king! [Substitute the word "king" as you need.]
Let him answer us when we cry out! (Ps 20 CEB)

CHAPTER 13

Psalm 9

IN PSALM 9 DAVID includes a mix of praise and petition and celebration and setback. Rather than giving into despair or questioning God's love/power, he affirms God's provision of hope for the downcast. So too, David reminds us that God is more powerful than our concerns for our struggles. In these, we can and should turn to God during them.

What's different from the other psalms we discuss in Part II is that David reminds us that even as we praise God and pray to God, we may still suffer. Yet, this shouldn't stop our desire to praise the God whose character never changes.

As you read, you can put yourself in David's place and insert your own "enemies," "nations," and "wicked," be they others, groups, or your personal demons and thoughts.

PSALM 9

> I will give thanks unto Jehovah with my whole heart;
> I will show forth all thy marvellous works.
> I will be glad and exult in thee;
> I will sing praise to thy name, O thou Most High.
> When mine enemies turn back,
> They stumble and perish at thy presence.
> For thou hast maintained my right and my cause;

Psalm 9

Thou sittest in the throne judging righteously.
Thou hast rebuked the nations, thou hast destroyed the
    wicked;
Thou hast blotted out their name for ever and ever.
The enemy are come to an end, they are desolate for ever;
And the cities which thou hast overthrown,
The very remembrance of them is perished.
But Jehovah sitteth *as king* for ever:
He hath prepared his throne for judgment;
And he will judge the world in righteousness,
He will minister judgment to the peoples in uprightness.
Jehovah also will be a high tower for the oppressed,
A high tower in times of trouble;
And they that know thy name will put their trust in thee;
For thou, Jehovah, hast not forsaken them that seek thee.
Sing praises to Jehovah, who dwelleth in Zion:
Declare among the people his doings.
For he that maketh inquisition for blood remembereth
    them;
He forgetteth not the cry of the poor.
Have mercy upon me, O Jehovah;
Behold my affliction *which I suffer* of them that hate me,
Thou that liftest me up from the gates of death;
That I may show forth all thy praise.
In the gates of the daughter of Zion
I will rejoice in thy salvation.
The nations are sunk down in the pit that they made:
In the net which they hid is their own foot taken.
Jehovah hath made himself known, he hath executed
    judgment:
The wicked is snared in the work of his own hands.
    Higgaion. Selah
The wicked shall be turned back unto Sheol,
Even all the nations that forget God.
For the needy shall not alway be forgotten,
Nor the expectation of the poor perish for ever.
Arise, O Jehovah; let not man prevail:
Let the nations be judged in thy sight.
Put them in fear, O Jehovah:
Let the nations know themselves to be but men. *Selah*
(Ps 9 ASV)

PART III

Thanksgiving: Gratitude, Joy, and Blessings

> You have turned my mourning into dancing;
> you have taken off my sackcloth
> and clothed me with joy,
> so that my soul may praise you and not be silent.
> O Lord my God, I will give thanks to you forever.
> (Ps 30:11–12 NRSVue)

For over three millennia Jews and Christians, both personally and in groups, have turned to the psalms of thanksgiving, singing, reading, and focusing deeply on God in tribute to the abundance in their lives ("my cup runneth over"; Ps 23:5).

When do you thank God and show gratitude? When do you experience God's joy? When do you bless God's holy name and thank God for the large and small blessings in your life? When do you bless others because sharing God's blessings to you extends them infinitely as you pass them on to others? When do you thank God for never-ending grace? I'm writing this the day after Thanksgiving and wondering how many of us carry our thoughts of God's many gifts into Black Friday and on into the push and pull of the Christmas season. I'll be the first to say that, although I try, I don't often keep up the fervor.

Yet, if we remember God's gifts only on Thanksgiving, Sunday morning, and/or during our daily prayer times, we miss the richness of *living in God* or *living in the Spirit*, however you want to think of it. To put it another way, we shortchange ourselves, God, and others. Unfortunately, most often we do this without realizing it.

While there's everything to gain by our special times of gratitude, such as at Thanksgiving, the goal of Christian living is to continue to thank God, show gratitude, recognize the joy in God's universe, accept God's blessings, and bless God and others continually. For if we accept God as the root of our being, then we must thank God in all circumstances (1 Thess 5:18–20). Otherwise, as we go through our busy days, we're prone to let it slip our minds, allowing our egos, activities, thoughts, and reactions take over.

In going back to what Paul meant by praying and giving thanks in all circumstances ceaselessly (1 Thess 5:16–17), let's remember that he wasn't asking us to say prayers 24/7 like thirteen-century cloistered nuns. Far from it—if we keep our heads down in deep prayer at all times, how can we spread God's goodness into the world? What he meant was for us to keep God in all our daily comings and goings.

The first I heard of what's now called the practice of deep gratitude was at lunch one day back in the early 2000s. I can't remember what got us into the conversation, but my friend Suzanne said, "I must be one of the most grateful people ever. I'm grateful for everything, all the time." Well, that set me back a bit because I'd never heard anyone come out and say such a thing. How could she be grateful for everything all the time? And wasn't that kind of boasting? She was a well-known Christian psychologist who'd attended seminary with me, so I didn't question her sincerity or willingness to say it out loud, but I was puzzled. It wasn't long afterwards that gratitude became a topic of interest, not just in religious circles but throughout our culture. Suzanne was merely ahead of the curve.

A major component of thanksgiving is receiving and offering grace. This can be tricky because if we don't accept in our deepest heart that God extends grace to us and to all the world, and if we don't graciously accept it, thanking God for it doesn't make much sense. Yet, as Dominic Done wrote in *Your Longing Has a Name*, "God doesn't demand your performance but invites you to rest in his inexhaustible grace. He accepted you and called you "beloved" before you were even born. In Ps 139:16 David voiced his wonder: 'You saw me.... My life was recorded in your book. Every moment was laid out before a single day had passed (NLT).' If true, he asks, 'How can I live out God's vision of who I already am?'"[1]

Part of the answer is to reflect on God's greatness and benevolence consciously as we go about our daily lives, stopping a second throughout the day to remember God in all things. At first this might feel contrived, even forced. However, if we lean into it and practice, it becomes automatic. There are days I'm better at it than others, but that's OK. Like Done indicates, God doesn't expect perfection in our attempts but to rest in grace daily.

In addition to thanking God by accepting and offering grace to ourselves and others, there's the component of accepting and giving blessings. In their beautiful book *The Lives We Actually Have*, Kate Bowler and Jessica Richie tell us:

> [A] blessing is more than a flush of gratitude for life's great gifts. Or a spiritual language for triumph.... The language of blessing is much wider and deeper. And it is woven throughout Scripture and the Christian tradition in a way that is far richer than previously understood. What is a blessing? It's [sic] most basic form, a blessing is a particular kind of spiritual act of speaking. (The term for blessing pops up in both Greek and Latin to mean "to speak well.") And most often, blessings are pleasing to the ear. They are a form of poetry that calls on God and stirs up the hearts of its listeners.[2]

You shouldn't be surprised that a huge component of psalms of thanksgiving is joy. It's a slippery word today because our culture is hellbent on attaining happiness. In *Aging in Spirit*, I explained

---

1. Done, *Your Longing Has a Name*, loc. 520 of 3262.
2. Bowler and Richie, *Lives We Actually Have*, loc. 271 of 480.

that happiness is "[a] state of high emotional pleasure. The magazines and blogs are full of why we are unhappy (that, itself, sets us up to be unhappy) and how to become happy when we're down. It's as if being anything but happy is unnatural—a social illness. But God's joy is no endorphin-fueled high brought on by trying the latest fad, buying more stuff, pushing our bodies to a physical high, eating delicious food, or having our kid get into Harvard."[3] These are good things for which we should be grateful—very grateful.

However, joy in God is a soulful, deeply profound feeling that all is well with our soul and with God despite what is happening in our lives. In this context, of the three types of thanksgiving psalms in Part III (gratitude, blessings, and joy), joy probably is the least understood.

Julian of Norwich illuminated what joy in God means when she penned the following words as she experienced life-defeating trials, including the Black Plague that killed between 30 and 50 percent of the population of Europe in the fourteenth century. Since then, thousands, perhaps millions, of people have clung to her message of ultimate joy in God as they struggle[d]. I certainly did as I slowly healed from the falls. The joy of knowing that no matter how things turned out I would be well in my soul sustained me. I mentioned earlier in the section on my story that even in my deepest despair, deeper down in my soul, I knew this. How God's joy works at the same time as human despair is far beyond our understanding. It just does!

From Julian:

> And so our good Lord answered
> to all the questions and doubts
> that I might make,
> saying comfortingly:
> *I may make all thing well,*
> *I can make all thing well,*
> *I will make all thing well,*
> *and I shall make all thing well;*
> *and thou shall see thyself*

3. Kaigler-Walker, *Aging in Spirit*, 135.

Psalm 9

that all manner of thing shall be well.
Where He says, *I may,*
I understand it for the Father;
and where He says, *I can,*
I understand it for the Son;
and where He says, *I will,*
I understand it for the Holy Ghost;
and where He says, *I shall,*
I understand it for the unity of the blessed Trinity;
three Persons and one Truth;
and where He says, *Thou shall see thy self,*
I understand the oneing of all mankind;
that shall be saved unto the blessed Trinity.
And in these five words
God wills we be enclosed
in rest and in peace.[4]

As you read the poems in Part III, notice how enjoyment, gaiety, dancing, singing, worshiping together, praying, thanking, and remembering God in times past, today, tomorrow, and forever are intertwined, resting on the never-ending cycle of love/grace/gratitude/joy and back to love, as we discussed in Part II.

To strengthen our commitment to steadfast gratefulness, some of us keep a gratitude journal, writing down our blessings. Others write their joys in living in God each day on slips of paper and place them in joy jars or boxes, where they can be pulled out later and read. At a retreat I co-led, we made joy jars. The jars ranked number one in our retreat evaluations.

---

4. Julian of Norwich, "POETRY."

CHAPTER 14

Psalm 95

In Ps 95 we find a call to worship, telling of God's greatness and omnipresence in our lives and asking us to worship by "making a joyful noise." It's perhaps the most explicit psalm about the link between God's joy and ours. You won't find any puritanical warnings of strife, fear, or an angry God who waits on high for us to slip up—no threats of fire, no brimstone—just pure joy. Again, it reiterates that we follow God because of God's grace, goodness, and love, not because we are commanded to.

To this end, we find five components of praise in Ps 95: shouting, worshiping, coming, knowing, and showing honor by bowing down.

PSALM 95

> Oh come, let us sing to the Lord;
> let us make a joyful noise to the rock of our salvation!
> Let us come into his presence with thanksgiving;
> let us make a joyful noise to him with songs of praise!
> For the Lord is a great God,
> and a great King above all gods.
> In his hand are the depths of the earth;
> the heights of the mountains are his also.

Psalm 95

The sea is his, for he made it,
and his hands formed the dry land.

Oh come, let us worship and bow down;
let us kneel before the Lord, our Maker!
For he is our God,
and we are the people of his pasture,
and the sheep of his hand.
Today, if you hear his voice,
do not harden your hearts, as at Meribah,
as on the day at Massah in the wilderness,
when your fathers put me to the test
and put me to the proof, though they had seen my work.
For forty years I loathed that generation
and said, "They are a people who go astray in their heart,
and they have not known my ways."
Therefore I swore in my wrath,
"They shall not enter my rest." (Ps 95 ESV)

CHAPTER 15

Psalm 100

PSALM 100 ONLY CONTAINS five verses, but there's a lot to unpack. Shout. Serve. Enter God's gate. Thank God. Bless God. God is good. God is everlasting love. God is faithful forever.

PSALM 100

> Shout triumphantly to the LORD, all the earth!
> Serve the LORD with celebration!
> Come before him with shouts of joy!
> Know that the LORD is God—
> he made us; we belong to him.
> We are his people,
> the sheep of his own pasture.
> Enter his gates with thanks;
> enter his courtyards with praise!
> Thank him! Bless his name!
> Because the LORD is good,
> his loyal love lasts forever;
> his faithfulness lasts generation after generation.
> (Ps 100 CEB)

CHAPTER 16

Psalm 138

PSALM 138 MAINTAINS THAT we who live close to God are the ones who live in reality, and those who believe in human power live in a world of fantasy. They simply don't know the joy and reassurance of having a personal, loving relationship with God. I especially love the line "The Lord will fulfill his purpose for me" (Ps 138:8).

PSALM 138

> I give you thanks, O LORD, with my whole heart;
> before the gods I sing your praise;
> I bow down toward your holy temple
> and give thanks to your name for your steadfast love
>   and your faithfulness,
> for you have exalted above all things
> your name and your word.
> On the day I called, you answered me;
> my strength of soul you increased.
>
> All the kings of the earth shall give you thanks, O LORD,
> for they have heard the words of your mouth,
> and they shall sing of the ways of the LORD,
> for great is the glory of the LORD.
> For though the LORD is high, he regards the lowly,
> but the haughty he knows from afar.

Though I walk in the midst of trouble,
you preserve my life;
you stretch out your hand against the wrath of my enemies,
and your right hand delivers me.
The LORD will fulfill his purpose for me;
your steadfast love, O LORD, endures forever.
Do not forsake the work of your hands. (Ps 138 ESV)

CHAPTER 17

Psalm 92

LIKE PSALM 138 IN the last chapter, Ps 92 speaks of the goodness and joy produced by praising God and the reassurance that God loves and will take care of us, in addition to reaffirming that those who do not live in God are the worse for not understanding the value of and valuing God's love and mercy.

PSALM 92

> How good it is to give thanks to you, O LORD,
> to sing in your honor, O Most High God,
> to proclaim your constant love every morning
> and your faithfulness every night,
> with the music of stringed instruments
> and with melody on the harp.
> Your mighty deeds, O LORD, make me glad;
> because of what you have done, I sing for joy.
>
> How great are your actions, LORD!
> How deep are your thoughts!
> This is something a fool cannot know;
> someone who is stupid cannot understand:
> the wicked may grow like weeds,
> those who do wrong may prosper;

yet they will be totally destroyed,
because you, LORD, are supreme forever.

We know that your enemies will die,
and all the wicked will be defeated.
You have made me as strong as a wild ox;
you have blessed me with happiness.
I have seen the defeat of my enemies
and heard the cries of the wicked.

The righteous will flourish like palm trees;
they will grow like the cedars of Lebanon.
They are like trees planted in the house of the LORD,
that flourish in the Temple of our God,
that still bear fruit in old age
and are always green and strong.
This shows that the LORD is just,
that there is no wrong in my protector. (Ps 92 GNT)

CHAPTER 18

Psalm 136

PSALM 136 OPENS WITH the same reminder to thank God that we find in so many others. Twenty-seven times the psalmist reminds us that God is good and will love us forever throughout both our highs and lows, ending with "O give thanks to the God of heaven, for his steadfast love endures forever." This last sentence creates a litany, much like what some of us read during Sunday or the repeated verses we sing in contemporary hymns. I find the repetition to be healing and soothing.

We likely can't relate to the historical accounts of God in ancient Israel in the poem. So, I again suggest you replace the historical events to key times in your life when God's presence carried you through. You might want to rewrite the psalm in your own words. Try substituting the word "grace" for "mercy." In their essence, they both speak of the same quality in God, but you might find one or the other conveys your understanding of God best in particular circumstances.

PSALM 136

Praise the LORD, for he is good;
for his mercy endures forever;
Praise the God of gods;
for his mercy endures forever;

Praise the LORD of lords;
for his mercy endures forever;

Who alone has done great wonders,
for his mercy endures forever;
Who skillfully made the heavens,
for his mercy endures forever;
Who spread the earth upon the waters,
for his mercy endures forever;
Who made the great lights,
for his mercy endures forever;
The sun to rule the day,
for his mercy endures forever;
The moon and stars to rule the night,
for his mercy endures forever;

Who struck down the firstborn of Egypt,
for his mercy endures forever;
And led Israel from their midst,
for his mercy endures forever;
With mighty hand and outstretched arm,
for his mercy endures forever;
Who split in two the Red Sea,
for his mercy endures forever;
And led Israel through its midst,
for his mercy endures forever;
But swept Pharaoh and his army into the Red Sea,
for his mercy endures forever;
Who led the people through the desert,
for his mercy endures forever;

Who struck down great kings,
for his mercy endures forever;
Slew powerful kings,
for his mercy endures forever;
Sihon, king of the Amorites,
for his mercy endures forever;
Og, king of Bashan,
for his mercy endures forever;
And made their lands a heritage,
for his mercy endures forever;

Psalm 136

A heritage for Israel, his servant,
for his mercy endures forever.

The Lord remembered us in our low estate,
for his mercy endures forever;
Freed us from our foes,
for his mercy endures forever;
And gives bread to all flesh,
for his mercy endures forever.

Praise the God of heaven,
for his mercy endures forever. (Ps 136 NABRE)

CHAPTER 19

Psalm 30

HISTORICALLY, PS 30 HAS been considered a prayer of thanksgiving by David after God brought him through a serious illness. Yet, it can be used after God has brought us through any crisis. Verse 5b, "Weeping may linger for the night, but joy comes with the morning," has become a mantra for those who suffer and lean on the hope of the dawning of a new beginning. You'll see that I've again chosen a modern version, this time The Living Bible, which fits our modern understanding.

PSALM 30

I will praise you, Lord, for you have saved me from my enemies. You refuse to let them triumph over me. O Lord my God, I pleaded with you, and you gave me my health again. You brought me back from the brink of the grave, from death itself, and here I am alive!

Oh, sing to him you saints of his; give thanks to his holy name. His anger lasts a moment; his favor lasts for life! *Weeping may go on all night, but in the morning there is joy* [italics mine].

In my prosperity I said, "This is forever; nothing can stop me now! The Lord has shown me his favor. He has

Psalm 30

made me steady as a mountain." Then, Lord, you turned your face away from me and cut off your river of blessings. Suddenly my courage was gone; I was terrified and panic-stricken. I cried to you, O Lord; oh, how I pled: "What will you gain, O Lord, from killing me? How can I praise you then to all my friends? How can my dust in the grave speak out and tell the world about your faithfulness? Hear me, Lord; oh, have pity and help me." Then he turned my sorrow into joy! He took away my clothes of mourning and clothed me with joy so that I might sing glad praises to the Lord instead of lying in silence in the grave. O Lord my God, I will keep on thanking you forever! (Ps 30, TLB)

CHAPTER 20

Psalm 105

PSALM 105 ISN'T OFTEN included among people's favorite psalms of thanksgiving. However, I have a specific purpose for including it. Although it was written to remind the ancient Hebrews of the need to praise God for building their nation over the centuries, it can serve as a blueprint for us to go back through our lives, note incidences, and be thankful for God's loving presence that brought us to where we are today. In workshops and retreats, the attendees and I either draw the history of God in our lives as a flowing river with twists and turns, cataracts, dry areas, and patches of still waters gently passing lush banks, etc.; make a timeline of the events; or write a story about them. You might want to give one of these a try, or create a personal adaptation of Ps 105.

PSALM 105

> O give thanks to the LORD, call on his name,
> make known his deeds among the peoples.
> Sing to him, sing praises to him;
> tell of all his wonderful works.
> Glory in his holy name;
> let the hearts of those who seek the LORD rejoice.
> Seek the LORD and his strength;
> seek his presence continually.

PSALM 105

Remember the wonderful works he has done,
his miracles, and the judgements he has uttered,
O offspring of his servant Abraham,
children of Jacob, his chosen ones.

He is the LORD our God;
his judgements are in all the earth.
He is mindful of his covenant for ever,
of the word that he commanded, for a thousand generations,
the covenant that he made with Abraham,
his sworn promise to Isaac,
which he confirmed to Jacob as a statute,
to Israel as an everlasting covenant,
saying, 'To you I will give the land of Canaan
as your portion for an inheritance.'

When they were few in number,
of little account, and strangers in it,
wandering from nation to nation,
from one kingdom to another people,
he allowed no one to oppress them;
he rebuked kings on their account,
saying, 'Do not touch my anointed ones;
do my prophets no harm.'

When he summoned famine against the land,
and broke every staff of bread,
he had sent a man ahead of them,
Joseph, who was sold as a slave.
His feet were hurt with fetters,
his neck was put in a collar of iron;
until what he had said came to pass,
the word of the LORD kept testing him.
The king sent and released him;
the ruler of the peoples set him free.
He made him lord of his house,
and ruler of all his possessions,
to instruct his officials at his pleasure,
and to teach his elders wisdom.

Then Israel came to Egypt;
Jacob lived as an alien in the land of Ham.

And the LORD made his people very fruitful,
and made them stronger than their foes,
whose hearts he then turned to hate his people,
to deal craftily with his servants.

He sent his servant Moses,
and Aaron whom he had chosen.
They performed his signs among them,
and miracles in the land of Ham.
He sent darkness, and made the land dark;
they rebelled against his words.
He turned their waters into blood,
and caused their fish to die.
Their land swarmed with frogs,
even in the chambers of their kings.
He spoke, and there came swarms of flies,
and gnats throughout their country.
He gave them hail for rain,
and lightning that flashed through their land.
He struck their vines and fig trees,
and shattered the trees of their country.
He spoke, and the locusts came,
and young locusts without number;
they devoured all the vegetation in their land,
and ate up the fruit of their ground.
He struck down all the firstborn in their land,
the first issue of all their strength.

Then he brought Israel out with silver and gold,
and there was no one among their tribes who stumbled.
Egypt was glad when they departed,
for dread of them had fallen upon it.
He spread a cloud for a covering,
and fire to give light by night.
They asked, and he brought quails,
and gave them food from heaven in abundance.
He opened the rock, and water gushed out;
it flowed through the desert like a river.
For he remembered his holy promise,
and Abraham, his servant.

Psalm 105

So he brought his people out with joy,
his chosen ones with singing.
He gave them the lands of the nations,
and they took possession of the wealth of the peoples,
that they might keep his statutes
and observe his laws.
Praise the Lord! (Ps 105 NRSVA)

PART IV

Lament: Loss, Pain, Grief, Fear, Questioning God, and Anger

> How long, O LORD? Will you forget me forever?
> How long will you hide your face from me?
> How long must I bear pain in my soul
> and have sorrow in my heart all day long?
> How long shall my enemy be exalted over me? (Ps 13:1–2 NRSVue)

Psalms of lament take the blue ribbon when it comes to numbers, with far more of them than any other type. This tells us that deep pain in the lives of David and the other psalmists was as common as it is today in ours. We've all known the feeling of circling the drain and needing to cry out for help.

The early Israelites, booth personally and as a people, were plagued with internal and external strife, breakdowns in relationships, losing their way, questioning God's actions, losing faith, illness, and death. Sound familiar? What's felt in the deepest level of our souls during these times of strife is grief. As we'll discuss below, even anger is undergirded by grief. You might want to think about that a minute. For doesn't the grief of losing someone dear to us or feeling frustrated with what's going on sometimes drive us to anger? Just look at the anger that swirled around the recent elections.

In *The Gravity of Joy: A Story of Being Lost and Found*, Angela Williams Gorrellep writes, "Grief is messy. It is runny-nose, tear-stained-cheeks, cry-in-a-ball-on-the-floor, can't-get-out-of-your-pajamas-till-noon, eat-and-drink-to-fill-the-soul-with-something-other-than-sadness, feel-like-you're-going-to-die-of-a-broken-heart messy. When your heart is broken you feel like the walking dead."[1]

What makes our stories tragic isn't what's happened or is happening. We know things happen. It's that too often, like after my falls, we can't believe it when they happen to us. "Why me?" "How could this have happened?" We forget, as Shannan Martin reminds us, "Jesus couldn't have been clearer about the inevitability of hardship, yet we are shocked when his promise rings true. When one of the gifts I'm handed looks like sadness, a lost opportunity, or something much worse, like suffering, I usually feel ripped off. I keep trying to barter my perceived obedience for the sweet life. Isn't this what I deserve? Isn't abundance best measured by the roses that grow, not the rain that grew them?"[2]

Here's another thought about grieving. Although we may believe we're circling the drain towards some serious hurt or disaster, we shy away from using the term "lament" because we don't understand it as David did: as a holy means of grieving. Maybe it suggests to us medieval saints daily lashing themselves with leather straps in repentance or modern-day pilgrims crawling the last few miles of their pilgrimage up to the Cathedral of Santiago de Compostela on bloody knees, sobbing as they wend their way to the shrine. However, these are extreme (and some would call psychotic) expressions of grief. That's not the interpretation we want to latch on to.

Below, two of my favorite quotes about lament flesh out some of the many sides of lamenting.

---

1. Gorrellep, *Gravity of Joy*, 75.
2. Martin, *Ministry of Ordinary Places*, 38.

"Wandering is a gift given only to the lost."[3] Well, if this isn't an odd quote! On the surface it seems self-evident. If we're not lost, why would we wander? However, this short statement is packed full of wisdom about how God relates to us and we to God in times of great loss or need. We know God doesn't cause us to be lost in pain and suffering—something else does: ourselves, others, unforeseeable circumstances, and random events. What we may forget is that God knows what it's like to live in this world and understands that we will get lost, wander, and cry out for help. So It's through our lamentations (grieving), not our stoic denials, that God will meet us and help us.

In her essay "I'm Black. I'm Young. I'm a Woman. And I'm Grieved.," Toni C. Butler writes, "Because I believe [that] when pain is silenced, [it keeps you silent]. So, we cry, plead, blame, beat our chests, hate, and/or take it out on others in a recurring cycle pain. Therefore, while we may not be able to eradicate what brings our pains, reading psalms allows the Holy Spirit to comfort, counsel and guide us." She adds, "Lament is crying out to God and expecting God to respond. It's individual and communal. It's an understanding that we can tell God about our troubles, and God won't leave us there. All lament should end in praise."[4]

In "What Does it Mean to Lament?," Lori Stanley Roeleveld explains, "In Hebrew, there are several words for lament or lamentation, but all convey the same sense of outwardly demonstrating deep sorrow or regret. In Hebrew, the lament definition is... to cry out, wail, [or] chant a dirge." She writes that lamentations are deeply embedded in the biblical tradition and serve multiple purposes:

1. **Expression of grief.**
2. **Repentance and seeking forgiveness.**
3. **Crying out to God in times of distress.**
4. **A form of protest and anger.**

---

3. Bauermesiter, *No Two Persons*, 48.
4. Butler, "I'm Black," 25, 28.

5. **Hope and trust in God.** Praise God, although to lament is to express pain and grief, it also encompasses elements of faith, hope, and love in relation to God's honesty, trust, understanding, and redemption. In this, when we lament, God blesses us, and we are blessed by God.[5]

In *The Lives We Actually Have*, Kate Bowler and Jessica Richie tell us:

> Blessed are you who feel things big. You who might feel embarrassment because of how overwhelming things can be. Blessed are you who need reminders that those emotions are not bad or good. They are just . . . information. You feel angry because this is unjust. You feel sad because this is awful. You feel tired because this is exhausting. Your emotions are not wrong or bad or lying to you or telling the full truth. They are giving you a bit of data that you shouldn't ignore. We love, and lose, and fall, and get back up, and fail, and try again.[6]

Thus, lamenting gives us the courage to name painful realities and to sit with them without attempting to escape them or jump to quick fixes so that we *can* get up and try again.

Finally, there is the anger component mentioned above. The psalmists didn't withhold either anger or tears of anger. In *The Fountain and the Furnace: The Way of Tears and Fire*, Maggie Ross writes, "The idea of tears washing anger from us is alien to the mores of power-oriented Western society. We are conditioned to justify our anger, to find the right place to put blame, and to always feel good about ourselves. Most of us associate anger and tears with tears that spring from anger, not tears that cleanse us from anger. But . . . tears of anger are themselves . . . a sign of choice, of potential change."[7] Thank you, God, that even the anger and tears we direct at God are cathartic, not abhorrent. They're nothing but the blessing we receive when we lament.

---

5. Roeleveld, "What Does It Mean to Lament?"
6. Bowler and Richie, *Lives We Actually Have*, loc. 357 of 480.
7. Ross, *Fountain and the Furnace*, 133.

PSALM 105

The following chapters are about taking our troubles, fears, and anxieties to God. A few are followed by modern psalms written by contemporary women, giving them a current meaning that's more relatable to us. After reading those not followed by another woman's interpretation, try writing your own. It's amazing how freeing the act of opening your pain, frustrations, anger, fears, and worries to God can be. Not only is it cathartic, but it's also another way of assuring you that God listens, cares, and stands with you.

CHAPTER 21

Psalm 13

PSALM 13 IS THOUGHT to have been written by David when Saul was trying to kill him and David had gone into a deep depression. We know this pain and depression. Someone you love(ed) and trust(ed) turns (or has turned) on you. It can feel like they are trying to kill you. Maybe you feel that they *have* killed a part of you. Maybe a piece of you wants to die. We've all suffered this to one degree or another. I certainly have. Only recently I found out that a woman whom I believed was a close, supportive friend wasn't at all who I thought she was but had been manipulating me all along to help her manipulate and control situations and other people. While this doesn't compare to having a husband or partner walk out or a child or other family member break your heart to pieces, it hurt. I was mad and sad, a bad combination if there ever was one, because together these two create a fight, flee, or freeze reaction that can end up in self-destruction. I felt used and disrespected. It took some fist-shaking at God, a couple of days of trying to understand why she had treated me this way, and cajoling my ego to back off and let God to settle me down, which God did with the double-barreled question, "How important is this to you in the grand scheme of things, and why?" I'm still hurt and wary of the person, but I'm neither holding it against her nor refusing to be in her presence.

PSALM 13

As you read Ps 13, notice how David exposes his aching soul to God, asks how long his trial will last, and ends by reinforcing and praising God for the steadfast love and blessings throughout his ordeal. You might want to remember back to a time of lamenting in your life and personalize the song.

PSALM 13

How long, O Lord? Wilt thou forget me for ever?
How long wilt thou hide thy face from me?
How long must I bear pain in my soul,
and have sorrow in my heart all the day?
How long shall my enemy be exalted over me?

Consider and answer me, O Lord my God;
lighten my eyes, lest I sleep the sleep of death;
lest my enemy say, "I have prevailed over him";
lest my foes rejoice because I am shaken.

But I have trusted in thy steadfast love;
my heart shall rejoice in thy salvation.
I will sing to the Lord,
because he has dealt bountifully with me. (Ps 13 RSV)

CHAPTER 22

Psalm 130

PSALM 130 IS AMONG the greatest pleas to God to bring us out of the depths of guilt, remorse, shame, and distress. Some theologians claim that David wrote Ps 130 after he was chastised by Nathan for capturing, raping, and then having her husband killed in battle when David learned Bathsheba was pregnant (2 Sam 12). Whether or not this is true, it makes the point that we can go to God with our deepest guilt and shame, and God will reconcile it.

Theologian David Guzik wrote, "As Luther struggled with the Satan at Coburg, he said to his companions, 'Come, let us sing that psalm [130], out of the depths, in derision of the devil.' . . . Surely this psalm is a treasury of great comfort to all in distress."[1]

Susan Williams suggested that we take a "closer look at what's going on in this psalm. 'Out of the depths I cry to you, O Lord!' It sounds to me like the psalmist has dug his own little pit, and there he sits, down in that pit, realizing exactly where he is, and the total impossibility of his situation. You know, when you're in a pit, it's a pretty isolating experience."[2]

You ever been in a pit? There are many kinds of pits: some more comfy than others, but no matter how severe, pardon the inevitable pun, they're just the pits. I've been there. Maybe somehow

---

1. Guzik, "Psalm 130."
2. Williams, "Love that Won't Let Go."

all your lovely props have been knocked out from under you—you used to think you knew what God had called you to do with your life, but suddenly, everything has changed. Maybe you find yourself stuck in the same old pattern of destruction you *thought* you were making progress with . . . but no, there you go again. Maybe your health has taken a cross-country hike and left you behind in the dust. Maybe you've lost someone dear to you. Maybe you feel totally isolated because you're a homeschooling mom, and adult company just can't happen because of the time you need to spend with your children, leaving you feeling isolated. Quadruple that during the COVID quarantine.

Williams goes on: "But God loves us so much, he even shows up right there IN our pit. Even when we think we don't WANT Him! He is Immanuel. God WITH us. There in the pit."[3]

That's pretty much where I was during the first couple of months after my third fall—in a pit. Thank you, Jesus, there were the psalms of lament to help me cope.

PSALM 130

> Out of the depths I call to you, LORD;
> Lord, hear my cry!
> May your ears be attentive
> to my cry for mercy.
> If you, LORD, keep account of sins,
> Lord, who can stand?
> But with you is forgiveness
> and so you are revered.
>
> I wait for the LORD,
> my soul waits
> and I hope for his word.
> My soul looks for the Lord
> more than sentinels for daybreak.
> More than sentinels for daybreak,
> let Israel hope in the LORD,

---

3. Williams, "Love that Won't Let Go."

For with the Lord is mercy,
with him is plenteous redemption,
And he will redeem Israel
from all its sins. (Ps 130 NABRE)

CHAPTER 23

Psalm 6

PSALM 6 WAS SUNG by the Hebrews as a prayer for recovery from grave illness. I felt the sting of not knowing whether I would live or die with both bouts of breast cancer. I wondered that if I lived, what would life be like from then on? Watching my mother slowly waste away and die from her second bout, I grieved for her and all who have walked cancer's painful path. As a survivor, I've supported, counseled, held hands with, and prayed with too many friends with cancer to count. This psalm is for us and anyone who has faced a severe crisis with no clear end.

Here again, remember that in David's day God was thought to undergird, and even cause, pains and ills. Now we know this isn't true, but let's be real. Sometimes in our crises we *do* feel like God has left us bereft to deal with them alone without explanation or comfort. Maybe we feel our ills are unjustified or know that they are. So, where is God? Without answers, we cry out.

Below is Ps 6 in its biblical form followed by my rewrite based on my cancers.

PSALM 6

LORD, do not rebuke me in Your anger,
Nor discipline me in Your wrath.

Be gracious to me, LORD, for I *am* frail;
Heal me, LORD, for my bones are horrified.
And my soul is greatly horrified;
But You, LORD—how long?

Return, LORD, rescue my soul;
Save me because of Your mercy.
For there is no mention of You in death;
In Sheol, who will praise You?

I am weary with my sighing;
Every night I make my bed swim,
I flood my couch with my tears.
My eye has wasted away with grief;
It has grown old because of all my enemies.

Leave me, all you who practice injustice,
For the LORD has heard the sound of my weeping.
The LORD has heard my pleading,
The LORD receives my prayer.
All my enemies will be put to shame and greatly horrified;
They shall turn back, they will suddenly be put to shame.
(Ps 6 NASB)

PSALM 6, MY ADAPTATION

Merciful God, do not leave me alone to deal with this cancer.
Be gracious to me, God, for I am confused by what I am facing;
Blessed One, heal me, for my emotional knees shake.
And my soul is sick with fear.

While you, God, seem nowhere near—for how long?

Hear me, God, and respond, save my life;
deliver me in the name of your steadfast love.

For even your Son, Jesus, asked why you had forsaken him.
Who else can I turn to?

I am tired of this worry;
every night I cry myself to sleep.

PSALM 6

I'm uneasy during the day.
Sometimes my sadness overtakes me;

I'm tired from the radiation.

Bless you, God,
for you heard my cries.
You heard my pleas for comfort;
you accepted my prayer for healing.
My my mind is at rest in you.
My scars will heal.

CHAPTER 24

Psalm 38

PSALM 38 IS A plea for repentance similar to Ps 130 in that scholars believe that David wrote Ps 38 in anguish and repentance after Nathan brought to light David's sin of raping and having Bathsheba's husband sent to the battlefront to be killed (2 Sam 12:7–9). By far, most people haven't transgressed so egregiously. Yet, as humans, we've all fallen short of how God wants us to live in one way or another and to one degree or another. It is here, when we don't stay on the path, that God offers the greatest measures of mercy and grace—God's love in action. It is here where we face our past ways and beg for this grace and love to restore us.

PSALM 38

O LORD, rebuke me not in your anger,
nor discipline me in your wrath!
For your arrows have sunk into me,
and your hand has come down on me.

There is no soundness in my flesh
because of your indignation;
there is no health in my bones
because of my sin.

Psalm 38

For my iniquities have gone over my head;
like a heavy burden, they are too heavy for me.

My wounds stink and fester
because of my foolishness,
I am utterly bowed down and prostrate;
all the day I go about mourning.
For my sides are filled with burning,
and there is no soundness in my flesh.
I am feeble and crushed;
I groan because of the tumult of my heart.

O Lord, all my longing is before you;
my sighing is not hidden from you.
My heart throbs; my strength fails me,
and the light of my eyes—it also has gone from me.
My friends and companions stand aloof from my
    plague,
and my nearest kin stand far off.

Those who seek my life lay their snares;
those who seek my hurt speak of ruin
and meditate treachery all day long.

But I am like a deaf man; I do not hear,
like a mute man who does not open his mouth.
I have become like a man who does not hear,
and in whose mouth are no rebukes.

But for you, O Lord, do I wait;
it is you, O Lord my God, who will answer.
For I said, "Only let them not rejoice over me,
who boast against me when my foot slips!"

For I am ready to fall,
and my pain is ever before me.
I confess my iniquity;
I am sorry for my sin.
But my foes are vigorous, they are mighty,
and many are those who hate me wrongfully.
Those who render me evil for good
accuse me because I follow after good.

Do not forsake me, O Lord!
O my God, be not far from me!
Make haste to help me,
O Lord, my salvation! (Ps 38 ESV)

CHAPTER 25

Psalm 10

WHILE PS 38 IS a plea for repentance, Ps 10 is a plea for God to heal our minds, bodies, and souls from the transgressions of ourselves, others (be they those we know or don't know), our society, or the world, and call evil ways to justice. It reminds me of the old African American hymn "There Is a Balm in Gilead (to Heal the Sin-Sick Soul.)" My soul has been sick from straying away from God at times, which is among the most excruciating sufferings I've experienced.

In addition to my personal crises, things going on around me in the larger world can make my soul sick with pain and anger. This is where Ps 10 stands apart from the others with its strong call for social justice. I'm thinking of the twenty-one innocent lives lost in the Uvalde school shooting. I grieve for the terrible price children pay during genocides and wars. They who are considered mere collateral by the perpetrators for their sinister purposes of power and greed are God's beloved children who deserve oh so much better. I grieve for those who suffer mental illness and weep for those who starve; are caught in the cycle of poverty; are held in bondage; are victims of domestic, sexual, and other violence; and who suffer from the evil effects of society's insidious sexism, racism, gender-ism, classism, lookism, ageism, elitism, ableism, and neurodiversity-ism.

Here again, let's remember we're not asking God to pitch evil doers into a fiery pit but to bring about a just and peaceful way of ending the suffering that they've caused. So, let's take another look at my earlier story about being at the *Los Angeles Times* Festival of Books and meeting the woman who wanted God to kill her husband and his mistress and pitch them into hell. Many women might have the same knee-jerk reaction immediately after a similar situation. But, girlfriends, her twenty-year desire for revenge is extreme and exactly what happens if we don't hear God's voice during our bad times. We are unable to allow the Holy Spirit to sit with us while we grieve deeply and then heal.

PSALM 10

> God, are you avoiding me?
> Where are you when I need you?
> Full of hot air, the wicked
> are hot on the trail of the poor.
> Trip them up, tangle them up
> in their fine-tuned plots.
>
> The wicked are windbags,
> the swindlers have foul breath.
> The wicked snub God,
> their noses stuck high in the air.
> Their graffiti are scrawled on the walls:
> "Catch us if you can!" "God is dead."
>
> They care nothing for what you think;
> if you get in their way, they blow you off.
> They live (they think) a charmed life:
> "We can't go wrong. This is our lucky year!"
>
> They carry a mouthful of spells,
> their tongues spit venom like adders.
> They hide behind ordinary people,
> then pounce on their victims.

Psalm 10

They mark the luckless,
then wait like a hunter in a blind;
When the poor wretch wanders too close,
they stab him in the back.

The hapless fool is kicked to the ground,
the unlucky victim is brutally axed.
He thinks God has dumped him,
he's sure that God is indifferent to his plight.

Time to get up, God—get moving.
The luckless think they're Godforsaken.
They wonder why the wicked scorn God
and get away with it,
Why the wicked are so cocksure
they'll never come up for audit.

But you know all about it—
the contempt, the abuse.
I dare to believe that the luckless
will get lucky someday in you.
You won't let them down:
orphans won't be orphans forever.

Break the wicked right arms,
break all the evil left arms.
Search and destroy
every sign of crime.
God's grace and order wins;
godlessness loses.

The victim's faint pulse picks up;
the hearts of the hopeless pump red blood
as you put your ear to their lips
Orphans get parents,
the homeless get homes.
The reign of terror is over,
the rule of the gang lords is ended. (Ps 10 MSG)

CHAPTER 26

Psalm 22

LET'S BE HONEST. MOST of us have been angry with God. "I'm hurt and angry about . . ." "I want answers as to what/why . . ." "If you're who you say you are, God, why don't you . . .?" "Why didn't you . . .?" "Where were you . . .?" "Did you see what happened?" "How could you . . .?" "That's not fair!" In response to this, Anne Lamott reminds us that a "fair is where the pony rides are."[1] But whether it's us ending up with the short end of the stick or witnessing terrible injustices we, like three-year-olds, cry, "God, that's not fair!"

There's no harm in being angry with and questioning God, for it means we trust our close, loving relationship with God enough to be honest in our emotions and accusations. God is big enough and cares enough about us to take on our raging pain. Reread this and think a minute. *God's love for us is encompassing and broad enough to hold our rage.* We can rest assured of this because know Jesus's first words on the cross.

As in other chapters, I've included a traditional and a modern translation so you can compare them with your understanding of what Jesus was telling us and asking God.

---

1. Lamott, *Somehow*, 99.

PSALM 22

My God, my God, why have you forsaken me?
Why are you so far from saving me,
so far from my cries of anguish?
My God, I cry out by day, but you do not answer,
by night, but I find no rest.
Yet you are enthroned as the Holy One;
you are the one Israel praises.
In you our ancestors put their trust;
they trusted and you delivered them.
To you they cried out and were saved;
in you they trusted and were not put to shame.
But I am a worm and not a man,
scorned by everyone, despised by the people.
All who see me mock me;
they hurl insults, shaking their heads.
"He trusts in the Lord," they say,
"let the Lord rescue him.
Let him deliver him,
since he delights in him."
Yet you brought me out of the womb;
you made me trust in you, even at my mother's breast.
From birth I was cast on you;
from my mother's womb you have been my God.
Do not be far from me,
for trouble is near
and there is no one to help.
Many bulls surround me;
strong bulls of Bashan encircle me.
Roaring lions that tear their prey
open their mouths wide against me.
I am poured out like water,
and all my bones are out of joint.
My heart has turned to wax;
it has melted within me.
My mouth is dried up like a potsherd,
and my tongue sticks to the roof of my mouth;
you lay me in the dust of death.
Dogs surround me,
a pack of villains encircles me;

they pierce my hands and my feet.
All my bones are on display;
people stare and gloat over me.
They divide my clothes among them
and cast lots for my garment.
But you, Lord, do not be far from me.
You are my strength; come quickly to help me.
Deliver me from the sword,
my precious life from the power of the dogs.
Rescue me from the mouth of the lions;
save me from the horns of the wild oxen.
I will declare your name to my people;
in the assembly I will praise you.
You who fear the Lord, praise him!
All you descendants of Jacob, honor him!
Revere him, all you descendants of Israel!
For he has not despised or scorned
the suffering of the afflicted one;
he has not hidden his face from him
but has listened to his cry for help.
From you comes the theme of my praise in the great assembly;
before those who fear you I will fulfill my vows.
The poor will eat and be satisfied;
those who seek the Lord will praise him—
may your hearts live forever!
All the ends of the earth
will remember and turn to the Lord,
and all the families of the nations
will bow down before him,
for dominion belongs to the Lord
and he rules over the nations.
All the rich of the earth will feast and worship;
all who go down to the dust will kneel before him—
those who cannot keep themselves alive.
Posterity will serve him;
future generations will be told about the Lord.
They will proclaim his righteousness,
declaring to a people yet unborn:
He has done it! (Ps 22 NIV)

Psalm 22

PSALM 22 FROM THE MESSAGE BIBLE

God, God . . . my God!
Why did you dump me
miles from nowhere?
Doubled up with pain, I call to God
all the day long. No answer. Nothing.
I keep at it all night, tossing and turning.

And you! Are you indifferent, above it all,
leaning back on the cushions of Israel's praise?
We know you were there for our parents:
they cried for your help and you gave it;
they trusted and lived a good life.

And here I am, a nothing—an earthworm,
something to step on, to squash.
Everyone pokes fun at me;
they make faces at me, they shake their heads:
"Let's see how GOD handles this one;
since God likes him so much, let *him* help him!"

And to think you were midwife at my birth,
setting me at my mother's breasts!
When I left the womb you cradled me;
since the moment of birth you've been my God.
Then you moved far away
and trouble moved in next door.
I need a neighbor.

Herds of bulls come at me,
the raging bulls stampede,
Horns lowered, nostrils flaring,
like a herd of buffalo on the move.

I'm a bucket kicked over and spilled,
every joint in my body has been pulled apart.
My heart is a blob
of melted wax in my gut.
I'm dry as a bone,
my tongue black and swollen.

They have laid me out for burial
in the dirt.

Now packs of wild dogs come at me;
thugs gang up on me.
They pin me down hand and foot,
and lock me in a cage—a bag
Of bones in a cage, stared at
by every passerby.
They take my wallet and the shirt off my back,
and then throw dice for my clothes.

You, GOD—don't put off my rescue!
Hurry and help me!
Don't let them cut my throat;
don't let those mongrels devour me.
If you don't show up soon,
I'm done for—gored by the bulls,
meat for the lions.

Here's the story I'll tell my friends when they come to
	worship,
and punctuate it with Hallelujahs:
Shout Hallelujah, you God-worshipers;
give glory, you sons of Jacob;
adore him, you daughters of Israel.
He has never let you down,
never looked the other way
when you were being kicked around.
He has never wandered off to do his own thing;
he has been right there, listening.

Here in this great gathering for worship
I have discovered this praise-life.
And I'll do what I promised right here
in front of the God-worshipers.
Down-and-outers sit at GOD's table
and eat their fill.
Everyone on the hunt for God
is here, praising him.
"Live it up, from head to toe.
Don't ever quit!"

Psalm 22

From the four corners of the earth
people are coming to their senses,
are running back to God.
Long-lost families
are falling on their faces before him.
God has taken charge;
from now on he has the last word.

All the power-mongers are before him
—worshiping!
All the poor and powerless, too
—worshiping!
Along with those who never got it together
—worshiping!

Our children and their children
will get in on this
As the word is passed along
from parent to child.
Babies not yet conceived
will hear the good news—
that God does what he says.

What is your take on this version? If it doesn't quite hit the mark, take a stab and write your own. The mere act of writing it will help you clarify your situation by, as they say, "getting it out of your system."

PART V

Wisdom, Guidance, Grace, and Understanding

> The spirit of the LORD shall rest on him,
> the spirit of wisdom and understanding,
> the spirit of counsel and might,
> the spirit of knowledge and the fear of the LORD.
> His delight shall be in the fear of the LORD.
> (Isa 11:2 NRSVue)

What comes to mind when you think of a wise person or someone who seeks God's wisdom? Maybe it's those rare souls who seal themselves from the outside world and turn to deep thinking and learning about God, such as Julian of Norwich? Or maybe those who practice Eastern religions, who meditate for hours on end on a mountain top? Or maybe Solomon, who asked God for wisdom above all else (1 Kgs 3:1–5; 2 Chr 1:7–12)?

You'd be right. All three are examples of seeking higher wisdom. They come to mind because we know about their dedication and accrued wisdom over the years. However, the only difference between them and us is that they're at a higher level of intensity than are we who ask God for wisdom in our daily lives. God doesn't set an intensity bar that we must meet or exceed to gain insight. James tells us, "If any of you is lacking in wisdom, ask God, who gives to all generously and ungrudgingly, and it will be given you" (Jas 1:5 CSB).

Girlfriends, that's *us*.

Asking for wisdom simply means going to God for advice; guidance; the ability to treat ourselves and others with dignity, love, and grace; and the ability to understand what is going on from God's perspective. Why? To develop spiritual stamina so that when a problem occurs, we don't have a knee-jerk reaction out of our emotions but out of wisdom.

Among the greatest gifts we receive when God shares wisdom with us is growing with ever-greater love and grace in our hearts and lives. On top of that, even if it's unintentional, we who grow in God's wisdom ooze God to the world. Merely saying hello, opening a door, or being kind to others may and can bless them like they've not been blessed in days, maybe weeks, months, or ever.

Recently I learned that when an underground stream that feeds a tree becomes saturated to the point of being unable to hold the water, the pressure forces the water back up into the tree where it will find a knothole as an escape valve. If no knothole is available, the tree can be damaged. In other words, the tree *must* share the water with its surroundings. There's a sermon in there somewhere, but let's not go there.

Photos of flowing trees are breathtaking. To me they depict how God, the ground of our being, floods us with so much wisdom that it can't help but push up through and out of us, and we become founts of blessings of love, mercy, and grace.

This reminds me of the old hymn "Come Thou Fount of Every Blessing." Although it was based on 1 Sam 7:12, it reflects the same desire for God's wisdom as expressed by the psalmists.

> Come, thou Fount of every blessing;
> tune my heart to sing thy grace;
> streams of mercy, never ceasing,
> call for songs of loudest praise.
> Teach me some melodious sonnet,

Psalm 22

sung by flaming tongues above;
praise the mount! I'm fixed upon it,
mount of God's unchanging love![1]

Other than for Ps 112, the final psalm in this part, there are no psalms that speak solely about wisdom. Our desire for God to hear us, help us, and guide our way is intertwined with praising, trusting, being grateful, and lamenting. I choose the early psalms in this part because the quest for God's wisdom is woven strongly into their overall purposes. Within each, I italicized the passages where the psalmist asks for or is grateful for God's wisdom.

Although our problems are different from the ancients asking for God's wisdom to help them stave off threats of being attacked by armies with arrows and wild beasts clawing them apart, metaphorically, the need is the same. Twenty-first-century slings and arrows still require God's wisdom and endurance in bringing them down. An example of when psalms can offer the grace of God in the twenty-first century (using twenty-first-century metaphors) is when I was in full combat with my two bouts of cancers. I leaned on the wisdom of the psalms and did active meditations with them. With the first I imagined God's army of Pacmen protectively gobbling up the cancer cells that had invaded my body. For the second I imagined God, like Captain Lightning, hurling electric bolts at the rogue cells until they were fried to a crisp.

---

1. Robinson, "Come Thou Fount."

CHAPTER 27

Psalm 51

ALONG WITH Ps 38, Ps 51 addresses David's transgressions with Bathsheba. However, here David goes beyond lamenting for his sins. After his lamentation, he asked God to clean and pardon him. Then he asked for guidance.

In this, he takes two steps. First, he asks God to teach him how to live. Second, he promises to teach others who have transgressed the same as he did. Modern stories abound about people coming clean with God after falling off the path and making a lifetime commitment to help other folks who're in the same situation. The best example I can think of is Alcoholics Anonymous (AA) and the spin-off groups for those who are addicted.

PSALM 51

> Have mercy on me, God, according to your faithful love!
> Wipe away my wrongdoings according to your great compassion!
> Wash me completely clean of my guilt;
> purify me from my sin!
> Because I know my wrongdoings,
> my sin is always right in front of me.
> I've sinned against you—you alone.
> I've committed evil in your sight.
> That's why you are justified when you render your verdict,

Psalm 51

completely correct when you issue your judgment.
Yes, I was born in guilt, in sin,
from the moment my mother conceived me.
And yes, you want truth in the most hidden places;
you teach me wisdom in the most secret space.

Purify me with hyssop and I will be clean;
wash me and I will be whiter than snow.
Let me hear joy and celebration again;
let the bones you crushed rejoice once more.
Hide your face from my sins;
wipe away all my guilty deeds!
Create a clean heart for me, God;
put a new, faithful spirit deep inside me!
Please don't throw me out of your presence;
please don't take your holy spirit away from me.
Return the joy of your salvation to me
and sustain me with a willing spirit.
Then I will teach wrongdoers your ways,
and sinners will come back to you.

Deliver me from violence, God, God of my salvation,
so that my tongue can sing of your righteousness.
Lord, open my lips,
and my mouth will proclaim your praise.
You don't want sacrifices.
If I gave an entirely burned offering,
you wouldn't be pleased.
A broken spirit is my sacrifice, God.
You won't despise a heart, God, that is broken and crushed.
Do good things for Zion by your favor.
Rebuild Jerusalem's walls.
Then you will again want sacrifices of righteousness—
entirely burned offerings and complete offerings.
Then bulls will again be sacrificed on your altar. (Ps 51 CEB)

Before we move on, let's consider the reference to unacceptable sacrifices. We don't sacrifice animals. What so many do, however, is live how they want while putting on a façade of being a follower of Jesus's teachings (i.e., bringing a fake self to God's altar). We can call this many things, but the word Jesus used is "hypocrite." Not acceptable! Instead of animals, God instructs us to sacrifice our selfish egos, desires to live as we want, and every other transgression on the altar, where they will be forgiven. This leaves us able to go forward, trying to follow Jesus's footprints as best we can with God's help.

CHAPTER 28

Psalm 1

I LOVE Ps 1. It speaks to the joy of living in God and all of creation and the delight of receiving God's wisdom. Time and time again joy bubbles up in me for no reason I can put my finger on. I can be sitting at my computer, reading a book, or taking a walk. Last week I was walking in our neighborhood with Jackie, the sock thief, for her daily sniff of the great outdoors. For so many months walking had been too painful for me to take her out. I was getting closer to being pain free that day and feeling the first hint of a cool breeze, a joy for early September in Texas. As we ambled along, I realized I'd made up a tune and was singing, over and over, "I love my trees, I love my God, and I love my knees." Pure, unadulterated bliss. I thought of David, who'd lived a life of pain, sorrow, fear, and uncertainty. Was this the bliss he'd felt at one those times when joy overtook him, and he created this psalm? I hope so.

PSALM 1

Blessed is the one
who does not walk in step with the wicked
or stand in the way that sinners take
or sit in the company of mockers,
but whose delight is in the law of the LORD,
and who meditates on his law day and night.

Women Living the Psalms

That person is like a tree planted by streams of water,
which yields its fruit in season
and whose leaf does not wither—
whatever they do prospers.

Not so the wicked!
They are like chaff
that the wind blows away.
Therefore the wicked will not stand in the judgment,
nor sinners in the assembly of the righteous.

For the LORD watches over the way of the righteous,
but the way of the wicked leads to destruction.
(Ps 1 NIV)

CHAPTER 29

Psalm 37

PSALM 37 GOES HAND-IN-HAND with Ps 1, as David expresses his delight and trust that God will wipe away his pain and lead him into joy. Note his reference to having and sharing God's wisdom in his old age as part of his euphoria. As I continue into my elder years, reading this passage gives me chills because of its joyous assurance that God is with me and with those with whom I've shared what I've learned over my lifetime of listening to and trying to live in God. It also reminds me of the many women of God on whose shoulders I stand. Thank you, Jesus!

PSALM 37

> Do not trouble yourself because of sinful men. Do not want to be like those who do wrong. For they will soon dry up like the grass. Like the green plant they will soon die. Trust in the Lord, and do good. So you will live in the land and will be fed. Be happy in the Lord. And He will give you the desires of your heart. Give your way over to the Lord. Trust in Him also. And He will do it. He will make your being right and good show as the light, and your wise actions as the noon day.
>
> Rest in the Lord and be willing to wait for Him. Do not trouble yourself when all goes well with the one who

carries out his sinful plans. Stop being angry. Turn away from fighting. Do not trouble yourself. It leads only to wrong-doing. For those who do wrong will be cut off. But those who wait for the Lord will be given the earth. A little while, and the sinful man will be no more. You will look for his place, and he will not be there. But those who have no pride will be given the earth. And they will be happy and have much more than they need.

The sinful man plans against him who is right with God. And he grinds his teeth at him. The Lord laughs at him because He sees his day is coming. The sinful have taken up their sword and their bow, to bring down the poor and those in need, and to kill those whose ways are right. Their sword will cut into their own heart, and their bows will be broken.

The few things that the man right with God has is better than the riches of many sinful men. For the arms of the sinful will be broken. But the Lord holds up those who are right with Him. The Lord knows the days of those who are without blame. And what is theirs will last forever. They will not be ashamed in the time of trouble. And in days when there is no food they will have enough. But the sinful will be lost forever. Those who hate the Lord will be like the beauty of the fields. They will be gone. Like smoke they will be gone. The sinful ask for something, but do not return it. But those who are right with God are kind and give. For those who are made happy by Him will be given the land. But those who are being punished by Him will be cut off.

The steps of a good man are led by the Lord. And He is happy in his way. When he falls, he will not be thrown down, because the Lord holds his hand. *I have been young, and now I am old. Yet I have never seen the man who is right with God left alone, or his children begging for bread. All day long he is kind and lets others use what he has. And his children make him happy. Turn from sin, and do good, so you will live forever. For the Lord loves what is fair and right. He does not leave the people*

Psalm 37

alone who belong to Him. They are kept forever. But the children of the sinful will be cut off. Those who are right with God will be given the land, and live on it forever. The mouth of the man who is right with God speaks wisdom. And his tongue speaks what is fair and right. The Law of his God is in his heart. His steps do not leave it. The sinful lie in wait for the man who is right with God, and want to kill him. The Lord will not leave him in his power. He will not let him be found guilty when he is judged. Wait for the Lord. Keep His way. And He will give you a high place to receive the land. When the sinful are cut off, you will see it.

I have seen a very sinful man spreading himself like a green tree in its home land. Then he passed away and was no more. I looked for him. But he could not be found. Look at the man without blame. And watch the man who is right and good. For the man of peace will have much family to follow him. But all the sinners will be destroyed. The family of the sinful will be cut off. But the saving of those who are right with God is from the Lord. He is their strength in time of trouble. The Lord helps them and takes them out of trouble. He takes them away from the sinful, and saves them, because they go to Him for a safe place. (Ps 37 NLV)

CHAPTER 30

Psalm 111

WE MIGHT THINK OF Ps 111 as a praise song, and it is. Yet, the last verse places it squarely in the collection of wisdom writings as it says, "The fear [high regard] of the Lord is the beginning of wisdom; all who live it have insight. His praise endures forever!"

Take a minute to reread and think about the passage before you read the psalm. To me it's among the most powerful verses in the Bible—loving, honoring, being led by, and trusting God is the entry to understanding, growing, and living in God. I'm not a big fan of tattoos, but if I were, I'd want this verse inked on my forehead!

PSALM 111

Praise the LORD!

I will praise the LORD with my whole heart,
in the assembly of the upright, and in the congregation.

The works of the LORD are great,
sought out by all who have pleasure in them.
His work is honorable and glorious,
and His righteousness endures forever.
He has made His wonderful works to be remembered;
the LORD is gracious and full of compassion.

Psalm 111

He has given food to those who fear Him;
He will ever be mindful of His covenant.

He has shown His people the power of His works,
that He may give them the inheritance of the nations.
The works of His hands are true and just;
all His commands are sure.
They stand forever and ever,
and are done in truth and uprightness.
He sent redemption to His people;
He has commanded His covenant forever;
holy and fearful is His name.

The fear of the Lord is the beginning of wisdom;
all who live it have insight.
His praise endures forever! (Ps 111 MEV)

Amen! And *amen*!

CHAPTER 31

Psalm 19

LIKE Ps 1, Ps 19 considers the magnificence of God's creation and reflects on the wisdom of God's laws. No wonder both have been referred to as "the psalms of the law." Remember, the Jewish faith is based on the covenant between God and Abraham that led to the laws that are recorded in Exodus, Leviticus, Numbers, and Deuteronomy. So, it was these laws that David points to as being perfect, the words of the laws as going into all the world, and that the wise words are simple, pure, and everlasting. These also are the laws Jesus would have known by heart as God's understanding of how we should live.

Whew, this is a lot to take in, and reading Leviticus, where most of the laws are written down, is as exciting as watching paint dry. Yet, understanding where Ps 19 comes from expands our understanding of David's message, as well as how it can apply to us living the psalms.

The last verse, "Let the words of my mouth and the meditation of my heart be acceptable to you, O Lord, my rock and my redeemer," are etched in my heart of heart. I repeat them before I begin to write or speak of or to God. You who've heard me speak may have wondered why I hesitate right before I start. Now you know.

PSALM 19

The heavens are telling the glory of God;
and the firmament proclaims his handiwork.
Day to day pours forth speech,
and night to night declares knowledge.
There is no speech, nor are there words;
their voice is not heard;
yet their voice goes out through all the earth,
and their words to the end of the world.

In them he has set a tent for the sun,
which comes forth like a bridegroom leaving his chamber,
and like a strong man runs its course with joy.
Its rising is from the end of the heavens,
and its circuit to the end of them;
and there is nothing hid from its heat.

The law of the Lord *is perfect,*
reviving the soul;
the testimony of the Lord *is sure, making wise the simple;*
the precepts of the Lord *are right, rejoicing the heart;*
the commandment of the Lord *is pure, enlightening the eyes;*
the fear of the Lord *is clean,*
enduring for ever;
the ordinances of the Lord *are true,*
and righteous altogether.
More to be desired are they than gold,
even much fine gold;
sweeter also than honey
and drippings of the honeycomb.

Moreover by them is thy servant warned;
in keeping them there is great reward.
But who can discern his errors?
Clear thou me from hidden faults.
Keep back thy servant also from presumptuous sins;
let them not have dominion over me!
Then I shall be blameless,
and innocent of great transgression.

Women Living the Psalms

*Let the words of my mouth and the meditation of my heart be acceptable in thy sight,
O LORD, my rock and my redeemer.* (Ps 19 RSV)

CHAPTER 32

Psalm 112

LIKE PREVIOUS PSALMS IN Part V, Ps 112 begins with David delighting in God. But then he moves into the impact that God's wisdom should have on our actions. In this, Ps 112 is a guide to spiritual development, living, and growth. Again, let's remember that these are same guides that Jesus lived by and taught. Talk about hitting the daily double.

PSALM 112

Praise the LORD!

Blessed is the man who fears the LORD,
Who greatly delights in his commandments!

His descendants will be mighty on earth;
The generation of the upright will be blessed.
Wealth and riches *will be* in his house,
And his righteousness endures forever.
Unto the upright there arises light in the darkness;
He is gracious, and full of compassion, and righteous.
A good man deals graciously and lends;
He will guide his affairs with discretion.
Surely he will never be shaken;
The righteous will be in everlasting remembrance.

He will not be afraid of evil tidings;
His heart is steadfast, trusting in the LORD.
His heart *is* established;
He will not be afraid,
Until he sees *his desire* upon his enemies.

He has dispersed abroad,
He has given to the poor;
His righteousness endures forever;
His horn will be exalted with honor.
The wicked will see *it* and be grieved;
He will gnash his teeth and melt away;
The desire of the wicked shall perish. (Ps 112 NKJV)

PART VI

Kinship

> Only kinship. Inching ourselves closer to creating a community of kinship such that God might recognize it. Soon we imagine, with God, this circle of compassion. Then we imagine no one standing outside of that circle, moving ourselves closer to the margins so that the margins themselves will be erased. We stand there with those whose dignity has been denied. We locate ourselves with the poor and the powerless and the voiceless. At the edges, we join the easily despised and the readily left out. We stand with the demonized so that the demonizing will stop. We situate ourselves right next to the disposable so that the day will come when we stop throwing people away.
> —Gregory Boyle, *Tattoos on the Heart*[1]

The warp and weft of psalms, those songs of the ancient Hebrews, the ones we rewrite to reflect our lives, and the ones we make up, like the silly ditty I created about knees and trees in Part V, are odes to God for the gift of allowing us to live in God's all-inclusive divine realm. In this, we live in right relationship with God, ourselves, our community, and all creation. For how else could it be? Kinship!

---

1. Boyle, *Tattoos on the Heart*, 190.

A lot of words are written each year about the importance of what the early writers called the kingdom of God. In the past several decades, Christians have begun using both the words "kinship" and "kin-dom" as being more descriptive of living in God based on the understanding that God lives in us, not in some far-away place, and doesn't rule us with the heavy hand of a king. Both words mean the same thing: we are the community of God's people living in community with God.

Because kinship is the raison d'être for the psalms and runs through them like a thread, we've got to tease out passages about kinship from them as we did with wisdom—except for one, Ps 119. Its entirety speaks of God's kinship. For this reason, it's the only one we'll look at in this part.

Believed to have been written by the prophet Ezra, Ps 119 is the longest psalm by far, with 176 verses, a cause for eye rolling for sure. Yet, once we get past thinking about the length, we find it to be among the most beautiful and instructive psalms in the book. It's believed to have been penned by an unknown author shortly after the Second Temple had been rebuilt (Ezra 5:1–7; 6:1–22) when peace seemed to be at hand. The poetry takes my breath away.

Beyond the beauty, the psalm praises God's loving relationship with us and all creation. It instructs us in how to keep God's ways and gratefully asks God to lead us, akin to Ps 23's "lead us not into our own desires but deliver us from going astray." Finally, the psalmist worships God as the Holy All-in-All. I could go on, but I want you to unpack the words for yourself—read them, let them soak into your soul, and pray the words along with the psalmist over and over until they become part of your very being. You will be blessed.

To get the most out of Ps 119, I have edited and broken it into parts, so you can digest one before you start into the next one. Always a workshop leader, I can see this being a multi-week class on Ps 119.

CHAPTER 33

Psalm 119

Blessed are those whose way is blameless,
who walk in the law of the Lord!
Blessed are those who keep his testimonies,
who seek him with their whole heart,
who also do no wrong,
but walk in his ways!
You have commanded your precepts
to be kept diligently.
Oh that my ways may be steadfast
in keeping your statutes!
Then I shall not be put to shame,
having my eyes fixed on all your commandments.
I will praise you with an upright heart,
when I learn your righteous rules.
I will keep your statutes
do not utterly forsake me!

[Pause]

How can a young man keep his way pure?
By guarding it according to your word.
With my whole heart I seek you;
let me not wander from your commandments!
I have stored up your word in my heart,
that I might not sin against you.
Blessed are you, O Lord;

teach me your statutes!
With my lips I declare
all the rules of your mouth.
In the way of your testimonies I delight
as much as in all riches.
I will meditate on your precepts
and fix my eyes on your ways.
I will delight in your statutes;
I will not forget your word.

[Pause]

Deal bountifully with your servant,
that I may live and keep your word.
Open my eyes, that I may behold
wondrous things out of your law.
I am a sojourner on the earth;
hide not your commandments from me!
My soul is consumed with longing
for your rules at all times.
You rebuke the insolent, accursed ones,
who wander from your commandments.
Take away from me scorn and contempt,
for I have kept your testimonies.
Even though princes sit plotting against me,
your servant will meditate on your statutes.
Your testimonies are my delight;
they are my counsellors.

[Pause]

My soul clings to the dust;
give me life according to your word!
When I told of my ways, you answered me;
teach me your statutes!
Make me understand the way of your precepts,
and I will meditate on your wondrous works.
My soul melts away for sorrow;
strengthen me according to your word!
Put false ways far from me
and graciously teach me your law!
I have chosen the way of faithfulness;

Psalm 119

I set your rules before me.
I cling to your testimonies, O Lord;
let me not be put to shame!
I will run in the way of your commandments
when you enlarge my heart!

[Pause]

Teach me, O Lord, the way of your statutes;
and I will keep it to the end.
Give me understanding, that I may keep your law
and observe it with my whole heart.
Lead me in the path of your commandments,
for I delight in it.
Incline my heart to your testimonies,
and not to selfish gain!
Turn my eyes from looking at worthless things;
and give me life in your ways.
Confirm to your servant your promise,
that you may be feared.
Turn away the reproach that I dread,
for your rules are good.
Behold, I long for your precepts;
in your righteousness give me life! (Ps 119:1-40 ESVUK)

[Pause]

May your gracious love come to me, Lord,
your salvation, just as you said.
Then I can answer the one who insults me,
for I place my trust in your word.
Never take your truthful words from me,
For I wait for your ordinances.
Then I will always keep your Law,
forever and ever,
I will walk in liberty,
for I seek your precepts.
Then I will speak of your decrees before kings
and not be ashamed.
I will take delight in your commands,
which I love.

I will lift up my hands to your commands,
which I love,
and I will meditate on your statutes.

[Pause]

Remember what you said to your servant,
by which you caused me to hope.
This is what comforts me in my troubles:
that what you say revives me.
Even though the arrogant utterly deride me,
I do not turn away from your instruction.
I have remembered your ancient ordinances, Lord,
and I take comfort in them.
I burn with indignation because of the wicked
who forsake your instruction.
Your statutes are my songs,
no matter where I make my home.
In the night I remember your name, Lord,
and keep your instruction.
I have made it my personal responsibility
to keep your precepts.

[Pause]

The Lord is my inheritance;
I have given my promise to keep your word.
I have sought your favor with all of my heart;
be gracious to me according to your promise.
I examined my lifestyle
and set my feet in the direction of your decrees.
I hurried and did not procrastinate
to keep your commands.
Though the ropes of the wicked have ensnared me,
I have not forgotten your instruction.
At midnight I will get up to thank you
for your righteous ordinances.
I am united with all who fear you,
and with everyone who keeps your precepts.
Lord, the earth overflows with your gracious love!
Teach me your statutes.

Psalm 119

[Pause]

Lord, you have dealt well with your servant,
according to your word.
Teach me both knowledge and appropriate discretion,
because I believe in your commands.
Before I was humbled, I wandered away,
but now I observe your words.
Lord, you are good, and do what is good;
teach me your statutes.
The arrogant have accused me falsely;
but I will observe your precepts wholeheartedly.
Their minds are clogged as with greasy fat,
but I find joy in your instruction.
It was for my good that I was humbled;
so that I would learn your statutes.
Instruction that comes from you is better for me
than thousands of gold and silver coins. (Ps 119:42–72 ISV)

[Pause]

Your hands made me and fashioned me;
Give me understanding, that I may learn Your
    commandments.
May those who fear You see me and be glad,
Because I wait for Your word.
I know, O Lord, that Your judgments are righteous,
And that in faithfulness You have afflicted me.
O may Your lovingkindness comfort me,
According to Your word to Your servant.
May Your compassion come to me that I may live,
For Your law is my delight.
May the arrogant be ashamed, for they subvert me with
    a lie;
But I shall meditate on Your precepts.
May those who fear You turn to me,
Even those who know Your testimonies.
May my heart be blameless in Your statutes,
So that I will not be ashamed.

My soul languishes for Your salvation;
I wait for Your word.
My eyes fail *with longing* for Your word,
While I say, "When will You comfort me?"
Though I have become like a wineskin in the smoke,
I do not forget Your statutes.
How many are the days of Your servant?
When will You execute judgment on those who
    persecute me?
The arrogant have dug pits for me,
Men who are not in accord with Your law.
All Your commandments are faithful;
They have persecuted me with a lie; help me!
They almost destroyed me on earth,
But as for me, I did not forsake Your precepts.
Revive me according to Your lovingkindness,
So that I may keep the testimony of Your mouth.

[Pause]

Forever, O Lord,
Your word is settled in heaven.
Your faithfulness *continues* throughout all generations;
You established the earth, and it stands.
They stand this day according to Your ordinances,
For all things are Your servants.
If Your law had not been my delight,
Then I would have perished in my affliction.
I will never forget Your precepts,
For by them You have revived me.
I am Yours, save me;
For I have sought Your precepts.
The wicked wait for me to destroy me;
I shall diligently consider Your testimonies.
I have seen a limit to all perfection;
Your commandment is exceedingly broad.

[Pause]

O how I love Your law!
It is my meditation all the day.
Your commandments make me wiser than my enemies,

Psalm 119

For they are ever mine.
I have more insight than all my teachers,
For Your testimonies are my meditation.
I understand more than the aged,
Because I have observed Your precepts.
I have restrained my feet from every evil way,
That I may keep Your word.
I have not turned aside from Your ordinances,
For You Yourself have taught me.
How sweet are Your words to my taste!
Yes, sweeter than honey to my mouth!
From Your precepts I get understanding;
Therefore I hate every false way. (Ps 119: 73–104 NASB1995)

[Pause]

Your word is a lamp for my feet
and a light on my path.
I have solemnly sworn
to keep your righteous judgments.
I am severely afflicted;
LORD, give me life according to your word.
LORD, please accept my freewill offerings of praise,
and teach me your judgments.
My life is constantly in danger,
yet I do not forget your instruction.
The wicked have set a trap for me,
but I have not wandered from your precepts.
I have your decrees as a heritage forever;
indeed, they are the joy of my heart.
I am resolved to obey your statutes
to the very end.

[Pause]

I hate those who are double-minded,
but I love your instruction.
You are my shelter and my shield;
I put my hope in your word.
Depart from me, you evil ones,
so that I may obey my God's commands.
Sustain me as you promised, and I will live;

do not let me be ashamed of my hope.
Sustain me so that I can be safe
and always be concerned about your statutes.
You reject all who stray from your statutes,
for their deceit is a lie.
You remove all the wicked on earth
as if they were dross from metal;
therefore, I love your decrees.
I tremble in awe of you;
I fear your judgments.

[Pause]

I have done what is just and right;
do not leave me to my oppressors.
Guarantee your servant's well-being;
do not let the arrogant oppress me.
My eyes grow weary looking for your salvation
and for your righteous promise.
Deal with your servant based on your faithful love;
teach me your statutes.
I am your servant; give me understanding
so that I may know your decrees.
It is time for the Lord to act,
for they have violated your instruction.
Since I love your commands
more than gold, even the purest gold,
I carefully follow all your precepts
and hate every false way.

[Pause]

Your decrees are wondrous;
therefore I obey them.
The revelation of your words brings light
and gives understanding to the inexperienced.
I open my mouth and pant
because I long for your commands.
Turn to me and be gracious to me,
as is your practice toward those who love your name.
Make my steps steady through your promise;
don't let any sin dominate me.

Redeem me from human oppression,
and I will keep your precepts.
Make your face shine on your servant,
and teach me your statutes.
My eyes pour out streams of tears
because people do not follow your instruction.

[Pause]

You are righteous, LORD,
and your judgments are just.
The decrees you issue are righteous
and altogether trustworthy.
My anger overwhelms me
because my foes forget your words.
Your word is completely pure,
and your servant loves it.
I am insignificant and despised,
but I do not forget your precepts.
Your righteousness is an everlasting righteousness,
and your instruction is true.
Trouble and distress have overtaken me,
but your commands are my delight.
Your decrees are righteous forever.
Give me understanding, and I will live. (Ps 119:105-44 CSB)

[Pause]

I call with all my heart; answer me, LORD,
and I will obey your decrees.
I call out to you; save me
and I will keep your statutes.
I rise before dawn and cry for help;
I have put my hope in your word.
My eyes stay open through the watches of the night,
that I may meditate on your promises.
Hear my voice in accordance with your love;
preserve my life, LORD, according to your laws.
Those who devise wicked schemes are near,
but they are far from your law.
Yet you are near, LORD,

and all your commands are true.
Long ago I learned from your statutes
that you established them to last for ever.

[Pause]

Look on my suffering and deliver me,
for I have not forgotten your law.
Defend my cause and redeem me;
preserve my life according to your promise.
Salvation is far from the wicked,
for they do not seek out your decrees.
Your compassion, Lord, is great;
preserve my life according to your laws.
Many are the foes who persecute me,
but I have not turned from your statutes.
I look on the faithless with loathing,
for they do not obey your word.
See how I love your precepts;
preserve my life, Lord, in accordance with your love.
All your words are true;
all your righteous laws are eternal.

[Pause]

Rulers persecute me without cause,
but my heart trembles at your word.
I rejoice in your promise
like one who finds great spoil.
I hate and detest falsehood
but I love your law.
Seven times a day I praise you
for your righteous laws.
Great peace have those who love your law,
and nothing can make them stumble.
I wait for your salvation, Lord,
and I follow your commands.
I obey your statutes,
for I love them greatly.
I obey your precepts and your statutes,
for all my ways are known to you.

Psalm 119

[Pause]

May my cry come before you, Lord;
give me understanding according to your word.
May my supplication come before you;
deliver me according to your promise.
May my lips overflow with praise,
for you teach me your decrees.
May my tongue sing of your word,
for all your commands are righteous.
May your hand be ready to help me,
for I have chosen your precepts.
I long for your salvation, Lord,
and your law gives me delight.
Let me live that I may praise you,
and may your laws sustain me.
I have strayed like a lost sheep.
Seek your servant,
for I have not forgotten your commands. (Ps 119:145–76 NIVUK)

Amen, and Amen!

PART VII

Conclusion

> Let us therefore approach the throne of grace with boldness, so that we may receive mercy and find grace to help in time of need.
> (Heb 4:16 NRSVue)

No matter what my condition or disposition, the book of Psalms offers a soft place to land. They're the prayers that ground me and allow me both to reflect on and contemplate the "now" of my everyday life and the strength I need to move forward with help from my trustworthy and approachable God. Similarly, in *I See You*, Terence Lester writes, "Everyone is looking for a safe place that feels like home."[1]

At home with God, we develop a never-ending, closer-than-close relationship with the Holy One—growing more trusting, loving the longer we're there. We're like the baby whom Maureen O'Brien described when a mother was being baptized and held her tiny daughter: "The baby reached with control, not recklessly waving her fist, not tapping her mother's face, not patting it, but a complete and full perfect reach, placing a tiny hand upon her mother's cheek."[2]

---

1. Lester, *I See You*, loc. 147 of 2715.
2. O'Brien, *What Was Lost*, 53.

I visualize the tiny baby looking deep into her mother's eyes with what she will come to know as trust, wonder, and hope, and the mother looking back with assurance and love. Kevin Nye calls this "unconditional positive regard—not unlike the way we understand how God loves."[3] If this doesn't catch your breath, I don't what would.

I return to the two psalms in this section, Pss 23 and 91, over and over. More importantly, I need them. For, as Beth Knobbe writes, "Sooner or later distraction gets the best of all of us, whether it comes in the form of emotional eating, power cleaning, exercise as an avoidance technique, or succumbing to the temptation of social media."[4]

For us women, I'd add getting distracted in routines with kids, partners, parents, women's groups, work, friends, and you name it. Think about what distracts you to the point that God fades from the scene. For me, it's either reading or writing, my ever-rambling thoughts, an art/craft project, or going on a trip. When it comes to planning a retreat or talk, I'm lost in another world—even when the topic is spiritual growth! Go figure!

This is why we need to move from just knowing that God is imprinted on our hearts to saying yes to *how* this imprint can direct how we live in the Spirit daily. If this were a race, the psalms would offer a clean, clear path, mile markers, medical aid workers, water stations, and our folks cheering us on. Our goal would be the safety, grace, love, and trust when we cross the line into really *living* in God. This might not be the best metaphor, but it gets the point across. Too many of us feel like we're on a race or maybe a treadmill 24/7/52 and need to include God to keep us going.

We know if we make the choice, God will be with us when we're aggrieved; overwhelmed; destitute; angry; in physical, emotional, and spiritual pain; confused; and stuck. We also can detect the Holy Presence in our delight, joy, soulful ecstasy, and when we're bubbling over with pure happiness. Yet, let's not forget that the Holy Spirit also is there in our mundane lives, when we're

---

3. Nye, *Grace Can Lead Us Home*, 79.
4. Knobbe, "From Desolation to Consolation."

Psalm 119

carpooling; cooking and washing dishes; giving a presentation; driving; resting; wiping little bottoms and snotty noses; covering a big meeting for a colleague who's out with COVID; being late and getting stuck in traffic; dropping an open jar of mayo on a clean floor (see my hand go up?); breaking a pinkie on the night stand; reading; visiting; attending meetings; taking the grands to the park; watching the sunset; tending to a mad toddler or belligerent teen; streaming a movie; working on a project; taking clothes to the dry cleaner; making love; having a glass of wine with a partner or friend; just sitting on your porch; drinking your morning coffee; listening to the birds; and whatever else happened to you today. God is everywhere in all circumstances.

CHAPTER 34

Psalm 91

I'VE SAID SEVERAL TIMES earlier that Ps 91 is my go-to psalm, my loadstone/North Star and compass, when I need God's presence. It helps me to lean into the guidance and comfort of the Holy Spirit in my darkest hours, as well as my daily life. No matter how often I read or recite Ps 91, and for whatever reason, I cannot stop myself from shedding tears of pain and joy each time.

Psalm 91 was penned in David's camp before going into battle. As in other psalms, David affirms that God will protect him. If you stand on the plain where the battle is believed to have been fought, you can look up into the hills and imagine God being there.

Psalm 91 has been named the "Soldier's Psalm." According to the Bible History Museum:

> In 1911, Winston Churchill faced a turning point in his career. He didn't know whether he'd be promoted or fired. His wife, Clementine, told him he needn't worry. That morning, she had come across some verses in Psalm 107 that read: "They that go down to the sea in ships, that do business in great waters; These see the works of the Lord, and his wonders in the deep."
>
> Clementine was convinced that her husband would be appointed head of the Royal Navy—which he was. A popular account from WWI tells of another psalm's long-standing connection to warfare. According to the story, a commander in the US Army's 91st Infantry

Psalm 91

Division gave each of his soldiers a card with the 91st Psalm printed on it. Soldiers took the cards into battle with the hope of being kept safe. When the actor Jimmy Stewart enlisted in the US Army Air Corps during World War II, his father gave him a letter and enclosed a copy of the same psalm. Over time, Psalm 91 has become known as the "Soldier's Psalm." Even in recent years, American troops in Iraq have been known to read it before going on patrol.[1]

I imagine my grandmother reading Ps 91 time and again as my dad was fighting in the South Pacific during WWII, was wounded, and remained in an Army hospital across the country for close to a year. My friend Poly made copies of Ps 91 and had them laminated for her nephews to tuck into their bags before deploying to Iraq.

The message of the psalm also fits the battles we face, such as physical conditions (cancer and similar life-threatening diseases), broken relationships, depression, addictions, and severe economic hardship. So too, it supports us in our daily trials, pains, and discomforts. I repeated the first two verses most nights as I recovered from the falls and slowly returned to my normal life.

You may have read this account of Ps 91 in *Aging in Spirit*, yet it's well worth recapping it here. My cousin Jill worked for the Red Cross in Houston when Hurricane Katrina nearly decimated New Orleans. Her unit was stationed at an airfield where the severely wounded refugees were helicoptered in. She said it looked like a scene from *M.A.S.H.*, with medical people, gurneys, and ambulances working together in organized chaos.

She and her team were assigned to meet buses, also pouring in by the dozens, with the less seriously hurt but nonetheless shocked, filthy, scared, and homeless refugees. Their job was to process these weary, dirty, and confused travelers and, after cleaning them up, disperse them to whatever facility they needed—medical, housing, etc. What brought Jill to her emotional knees was that as the buses arrived and unloaded, often the people would

1. Museum of the Bible.

be chanting the Ninety-First Psalm. Like the displaced and fearful David, they were assuring themselves that God was with them no matter their future. Jill went home and reread the Ninety-First Psalm.

PSALM 91

He that dwelleth in the secret place of the most High
shall abide under the shadow of the Almighty.

I will say of the LORD, *He is* my refuge and my fortress:
my God; in him will I trust.
Surely he shall deliver thee from the snare of the fowler,
and from the noisome pestilence.
He shall cover thee with his feathers,
and under his wings shalt thou trust:
his truth *shall be thy* shield and buckler.
Thou shalt not be afraid for the terror by night;
nor for the arrow *that* flieth by day;
nor for the pestilence *that* walketh in darkness;
nor for the destruction *that* wasteth at noonday.
A thousand shall fall at thy side,
and ten thousand at thy right hand;
but it shall not come nigh thee.

Only with thine eyes shalt thou behold
and see the reward of the wicked.
Because thou hast made the LORD, *which is* my refuge,
even the most High, thy habitation;
there shall no evil befall thee,
neither shall any plague come nigh thy dwelling.
For he shall give his angels charge over thee,
to keep thee in all thy ways.
They shall bear thee up in *their* hands,
lest thou dash thy foot against a stone.
Thou shalt tread upon the lion and adder:
the young lion and the dragon shalt thou trample under feet.

Because he hath set his love upon me, therefore will I deliver
  him:

Psalm 91

I will set him on high, because he hath known my name.
He shall call upon me, and I will answer him:
I *will be* with him in trouble;
I will deliver him, and honour him.
With long life will I satisfy him,
and shew him my salvation. (Ps 91 AKJV)

CHAPTER 35

Psalm 23

FINALLY, WE TALK ABOUT the beloved Twenty-Third Psalm. As a research nerd, I tried to count the number of books on Amazon devoted to it and gave up. Google was no help, either. All anyone can say is that the passage has deeply touched more lives than any other in either Testament.

1960s freedom fighter, speaker, and author Fannie Lou Hamer penned, "I never know today what's going to happen to me tonight, but I do know as I walk alone, I walk with my hand in God's hand."[1] She told an audience, "I have walked through the shadows of death because it was on the tenth of September in '62 when they shot sixteen times in a house and it wasn't a foot over the bed where my head was."[2] Clearly, this brave woman lived the Twenty-Third Psalm as she stood at the forefront one of the most tragic yet formidable eras of the twentieth century. In so doing she helped shape the outcome of the Civil Rights Movement.

In a totally different way, my dad's mother exercised with a morning routine she created to assure that she got both her daily exercise and Ps 23. This is no joke; you can't make up this kind of stuff. This was back in the early 1950s, and she was in her late seventies. Around 5 o'clock each morning, you could find her in

---

1. Holmes, *Joy Unspeakable*, 126–27.
2. Holmes, *Joy Unspeakable*, 125.

PSALM 23

the kitchen, fully dressed, saying, "The Lord (kick one leg out) is my shepherd (kick the other leg out), I (shadow punch one arm) shall (shadow punch) not (shadow punch) want (shadow punch)!" Had she not lived the rest of her day, her life, in the spirit of the psalms, this would have been ridiculous. But it wasn't. It was her!

Savannah Guthrie tells us in *Mostly What God Does*, "Psalm 23 is everybody's psalm. It is famous for a reason, holding interest and relevance across time and generations, capable of interpretation and reinterpretation. It is the Bible's Mona Lisa; walk a few steps to the side of it and you may see it in an entirely different light. Whole books have been dedicated to its captivating passages."[3]

In closing, let's look and learn from this best-loved psalm, first in the KJV, the most popular and the one most of us learned and recited in Sunday school, followed by a personal adaptation by a Facebook friend.

PSALM 23

The LORD is my shepherd; I shall not want.

He maketh me to lie down in green pastures: he leadeth me beside the still waters.

He restoreth my soul: he leadeth me in the paths of righteousness for his name's sake.

Yea, though I walk through the valley of the shadow of death, I will fear no evil: for thou art with me; thy rod and thy staff they comfort me.

Thou preparest a table before me in the presence of mine enemies: thou anointest my head with oil; my cup runneth over.

Surely goodness and mercy shall follow me all the days of my life: and I will dwell in the house of the LORD for ever. (Ps 23 KJV)

---

3. Guthrie, *Mostly What God Does*, 93.

Women Living the Psalms

Psalm 23: Personalized by Terri Harmon Leander

The Lord is my Shepherd.
I lack for nothing.
On the contrary, you, Lord,
Lead me to enjoy
a good and full life
in peace of mind
And abundance.
You make me to lie down
in green, lush woods
at Breakheart Reservation,
Content and secure,
Fully knowing, [sic]
I am one of Your beloved children.
You lead me beside
the ebb and flow of the tides,
along Nahant Beach,
Where the heavens
meet the sea at the horizon;
And you manifest for me
All that will make my life flourish,
Providing me with well being
And financial prosperity.
You renew my spirit
for this new life of my journey,
Along the right paths;
The paths that lead
and call my soul
In covenant with You, O Lord,
So that I may serve you completely
in living the Love and Justice
of Jesus,
bringing honor to Your holy name.
Even though, [sic] I have walked
a lifetime in the darkest valleys,
As a victim of tragic circumstances,
At the hands of others,
who put ego and self
before You
to harm me,

Psalm 23

I no longer feel
that evil lurking, [sic]
that surrounded me,
And clouded my vision
And deeply wounded my self worth [sic].
From that dark valley,
I know now,
You have rescued me;
You will guide, protect,
reassure and support me,
As I walk this yet trodden road
that leads me closer
to You.
Praise you, O Lord!
As you have prepared for me
A feast;
A table set extravagantly before me,
A life from this point onward,
where I will no longer
just survive,
But thrive.
No longer will the pain
of the disdain of others
Be a burden on my heart.
You have anointed me,
Called me by name
To Love and Serve You.
Surely, Your goodness
and steadfast love
Will surround me
for the rest of my days
And I shall dwell in You,
And You in me,
forever more.[4]

---

4. Leander, "Psalm 23."

Benediction

As we reach the end of our journey through the psalms, I leave you with my favorite benediction. Based on Num 6:24–26, Rev. Robert Schuller recited it each Sunday at the end of his sermon. Each time I heard him, I felt blessed, indeed.

> And now may the Lord bless you and keep you. May the Lord make His face to shine upon you and be gracious unto you. And may God give you His peace in your going out and in your coming in, in your lying down and in your rising up, in your labor and in your leisure, in your laughter and in your tears . . . Until you come to stand before Jesus in that day in which there is no sunset and no dawning. Amen.[5]

---

5. CKRON, "Famous Benediction."

Epilogue

TODAY I'M A COUPLE of days short of a year since my first fall, and I'm sending the final draft of *Women Living the Psalms* to my publisher. If someone had told me the morning of the fall how 2024 and the book would turn out I would have said, maybe bemusedly, "No way," and given them every reason why. Well, "*Way!*"

Would I have chosen the happenings of 2024? Of course not. Would I go back now and change them if I could? That's a hard question. My immediate reaction might be "yes" because of the disruption and pain. Yet the answer is a solid "no." I've lived a year closer to God than any other in my life. I now know more about me than ever before. Best of all, I've been given and have given more love to all of God's creation than ever before.

While I'm not convinced that everything that happens to us is for a reason, I know in my heart that God provides the way for us to handle every situation to the best possible outcome with love, concern, and guidance. In my case, the way was having the book of Psalms by my side. Notice I didn't say God would take care of a situation or remove it but that God would help us handle what comes to us if we live the psalms. Just look at David's messy life. What living the psalms will do is allow us to partner with God as situations unfold.

Today I'm in physical therapy three times a week, have only a little pain, and am ready to get back to having a good life with Bud and my friends, all the while continuing God's work in 2025. I started 2024 crying "Oh God!" I end it by shouting, "Thank you, Jesus!"

Activities for Individuals and Groups

SIMPLY HEARING OR READING something won't hang around or impact your life much without "getting it out there" in one way or another. This is a major reason why we thrive on women's groups, where we talk through each other's joys, concerns, and pains. Here, we clarify our thinking and make decisions, get things off our chests, and feel supported. It's why every workshop on leading women's groups I've attended all but demands that we give attendees time to work in groups to help process and personalize what a speaker or panel has presented.

As I mentioned in *Aging in Spirit*, a group can be anything from having a few close girlfriends who serve as supports for each other to an international chat group to organized groups, such as a church group or the United Women of Faith. If you don't have a group, try to join one or create your own.

Another way to process and learn from what you've read or been thinking is by journaling. Believe it or not, keeping a record of one's thoughts is as old as writing itself. It's probably shaped Christianity more than any single form of writing other than Paul's letters. Think of Augustine, Thomas Aquinas, Martin Luther, and Julian of Norwich, among others, who wrote down what they were thinking. While we don't stand with these giants of Christianity, the value of writing about our spiritual journey is the same. It helps us clear our minds by getting ideas, emotions, and questions down on paper.

We also embed information by creating something visual through artwork/crafts. The first rule here is, don't think you can't. You can. Too often our society smothers artistic interest in children. Mother told of sitting next to a grandfather and grandson on an airplane. As the boy worked away with his crayons and a coloring book, the whole time the grandfather told him, "Color within the lines; you got to stay within the lines. The sun isn't green, it's yellow. People don't have purple faces." Finally, the boy put away his things, and Mother wanted to cry. These restrictions to our natural creativity can impact us throughout our lives.

Similarly, as we grow past childhood, perfectionism begins to raise its demon head, and we start to compare our work with others—another killer of the pure joy of using our eyes and hands to express our relationship with our world. God doesn't expect us to excel in these efforts, but to try.

So, put your fears away and try some of the activities below.

WRITING

After reading each Part in this book, ask yourself these questions. Before you begin, invite the Holy Spirit to be with you and guide you as you contemplate each. Then either write them down or create something (see below for suggestions). I often combine them by drawing in my journal.

1. What resonated with me in the psalms? Are there specific psalms or verses that really grabbed me? Why? How will this help me day by day?

2. Did any idea, psalm, or specific verses upset me? Why? Spending time with your response can help you sort out difficulties or conflicts you likely have had, have now, or will have in the future in the area.

3. How can I incorporate the psalm into my everyday life so that I walk closer with God in all things?

ACTIVITIES FOR INDIVIDUALS AND GROUPS

4. Bless God after each session, giving thanks for the insight you received and guidance as you continue forward.

ACTIVITIES

1. Journal and/or write poems, prayers, or songs.
2. Express what you're feeling by drawing, painting, making three-dimensional objects, playing with clay, and/or any media available. Don't forget the fiber/fabric arts such as crocheting, knitting, quilt making, and sewing wall hangings.
3. Make a collage about your feelings after you read a single psalm or whole Part in this book. The Retreat House and Spirituality Center in Richardson, Texas, has a room devoted to tables where thousands of cutout pictures from everything from old issues of *National Geographic* to current catalogs are nicely stacked into categories. We use them to create a work that expresses us on paper. What we create depends on the topic of the workshop or class. I love collages because they're a perfect way to lose myself in expressing myself with pictures, scissors, and glue with no distractions, such as having to plan, draw, or choose colors.
4. A powerful activity for digging deep into your soul is coloring mandalas. You can either download a mandala outline or buy a coloring book of mandalas that you can fill in yourself. In workshops, we usually ask a question for attendees to ponder, fill in a mandala, and then share them with the group.

    Meditating on a mandala that is complete is another way of using them to bring up insight. This is an ancient use of color, space, and design for worship, akin to walking a labyrinth.

I could go on for pages, but I suggest you search for methods of bringing your relationship with God to light that suit you. I also suggest you try others that don't (drawing if you're primarily and writer, etc.). Pushing ourselves a little beyond our comfort zones often brings new understandings.

Whatever you choose, do it with an open mind and heart, and listen for God.

Bibliography

Arthur, Alura. *Briefly Perfectly Human: Making an Authentic Life by Getting Real About the End*. New York: Mariner, 2024.
Bauermeister, Erica. *No Two Persons: A Novel*. New York: St. Martin's Griffin, 2013.
Bender, Aimee. *The Particular Sadness of Lemon Cake: A Novel*. New York: Random House, 2010.
Berthier, Jacques. "Bless the Lord, My Soul." Catholic Hymn. http://catholichymn.blogspot.com/2015/09/Bless-the-Lord-My-Soul.html.
Bessy, Sarah. *Miracles and Other Reasonable Things: A Story of Unlearning and Relearning God*. New York: Howard, 2019. Kindle.
Bowler, Kate, and Jessica Richie. *The Lives We Actually Have*. New York: Convergent, 2023. Kindle.
Butler, Tori C. "I'm Black, I'm Young, I'm a Woman, and I'm Grieved." In *I'm Black. I'm Christian. I'm Methodist.*, edited by Lillian C. Smith et al., 16–28. Nashville: Abingdon, 2020.
CKRON. "The Famous Benediction of Robert Schuller." http://www.ckron.com/rs8.htm.
Cooke, George William. "I've Got the Joy, Joy, Joy Down in My Heart." Hymnary.org. https://hymnary.org/tune/i_have_the_joy_joy_joy_joy_cooke.
Crosby, Fanny J. "Blessed Assurance." Wikipedia. https://en.wikipedia.org/wiki/Blessed_Assurance.
Cudjoe-Wilkes, Gabby, and Andrew Wilkes. *Psalms for Black Lives: Reflections for the Work of Liberation*. Nashville: Upper Room, 2022.
Davis, Ellen F. *Getting Involved with God: Rediscovering the Old Testament*. Lanham, MD: Cowley, 2001. Kindle.
deClaisse-Walford, Nancy L., et al. *The Book of Psalms*. New International Commentary on the Old Testament. Grand Rapids: Eerdmans, 2014.
Done, Dominic. *Your Longing Has a Name: Come Alive to the Story You Were Made For*. Nashville: Thomas Nelson, 2023. Kindle.
Frost, Robert. "The Road Not Taken." In *An Introduction to American Poetry*, edited by Frederick C. Prescott and Gerald D. Sanders. New York: F. S. Crofts, 1946.

Bibliography

Gorrell, Angela Williams. *The Gravity of Joy: A Story of Being Lost and Found.* Grand Rapids: Eerdmans, 2021.

Guthrie, Savannah. *Mostly What God Does: Reflections on Seeking and Finding His Love Everywhere.* Grand Rapids: Eerdmans. 2021.

Guzik, David. "Psalm 130—Out of the Depths." Enduring Word. https://enduringword.com/bible-commentary/psalm-130.

———. "Psalm 16—The Benefits of a Life-Commitment to God." Enduring Word. https://enduringword.com/bible-commentary/psalm-16/.

Holmes, Barbara A. *Joy Unspeakable: Contemplative Practices of the Black Church.* 2nd ed. Minneapolis: Fortress, 2017.

Jeremiah, David. "What the Book of Psalms Is All About." David Jeremiah. https://davidjeremiah.blog/what-the-book-of-psalms-is-all-about/.

Julian of Norwich. "POETRY: All Shall Be Well, by Julian of Norwich." The Value of Sparrows. https://thevalueofsparrows.wordpress.com/2016/11/30/poetry-all-shall-be-well-by-julian-of-norwich.

Kaigler-Walker, Karen. *Aging in Spirit: A Woman's Journey to God.* Eugene, OR: Resource, 2023.

———. *Positive Aging: Every Woman's Quest for Wisdom and Beauty.* Berkeley, CA: Canari, 1997.

Knobbe, Beth. "From Desolation to Consolation: Distraction—The Movement to Focus." Ignatian Ministries, September 15, 2024. https://ignatianministries.org/into-the-deep-blog/fromdesolationtoconsolation_distractionthemovementtofocus.

Lamott, Anne. *Somehow: Thoughts on Love.* New York: Riverhead, 2024.

Lester, Terence. *I See You: How Love Opens Our Eyes to Invisible People.* Downers Grove, IL: InterVarsity, 2019.

Martin, Shannon. *The Ministry of Ordinary Places: Waking Up to God's Goodness Around You.* Nashville: Thomas Nelson. 2018.

Merrill, Nan C. *Psalms for Praying: An Invitation to Wholeness.* 10th ann. ed. London: Bloomsbury, 2016.

Moss III, Otis. "The Gospel and the Blues." *Richard Rohr's Daily Meditations.* Center for Action and Contemplation, January 18, 2024. https://email.cac.org/t/d-e-vujllkd-iuklkdwjh-g/.

Museum of the Bible. "Psalm 91: The Soldier's Psalm." May 3, 2021. https://www.museumofthebible.org/book-minute/psalm-91.

Niequest, Shauna. *Present Over Perfect: Leaving Behind Frantic for a Simpler, More Soulful Way of Living.* Grand Rapids: Zondervan, 2016.

Nye, Kevin. *Grace Can Lead Us Home: A Christian Call to End Homelessness.* Huntington, IN: Harold, 2022.

O'Brien, Maureen. *What Was Lost: Seeking Refuge in the Psalms.* Cincinnati, OH: Franciscan, 2021.

Onwuchekwa, John. *We Go On: Finding Purpose in All of Life's Sorrows and Joys.* Grand Rapids: Zondervan, 2022. Kindle.

Postiff, Matt. "Categorizing the Psalms." Fellowship Bible Church, November 25, 2014. https://www.fbcaa.org/MAPBlog/PsalmsCategories.pdf.

Bibliography

Quart, Alissa. *Bootstrapped: Liberating Ourselves from the American Dream.* New York: HarperCollins, 2023.

Rhodes, Julie K. *Chronic Grace: Prayers, Saints, and Thorns that Stay.* Las Vegas: Leadership. 2023.

Robinson, Robert. "Come Thou Fount of Every Blessing." United Methodist Hymnal. United Methodist, 1989, 400.

Roeleveld, Lori Stanley. "What Does It Mean to Lament? Bible Meaning Explained." Crosswalk, May 9, 2024. https://www.crosswalk.com/faith/bible-study/what-is-a-lament-in-the-bible.html.

Rohr, Richard. "The Prophetic Path: Motivated by Love." *Richard Rohr's Daily Meditations.* Center for Action and Contemplation, November 26, 2023. https://cac.org/?s=The+prophetic+path+motivated+by+love&post_type=post&cat=1.

Ross, Maggie. *The Fountain and the Furnace: The Way of Tears and Fire.* Mahwah, NJ: Paulist, 1987.

Rufner, David. "The Psalms on His Lips." 1517.org, April 25, 2019. https://www.1517.org/articles/the-psalms-on-his-lips#:~:text=Jesus%20died%20with%20a%20Psalm,other%20Psalms%20upon%20His%20lips.

Sabatella, Matthew. "This Little Light of Mine: About the Song." Ballad of America. https://balladofamerica.org/this-little-light-of-mine/#song-history.

Salsbery, Stacey. "20 Benefits of Being in God's Word According to Psalm 119." Revive Our Hearts, January 1, 2024. https://www.reviveourhearts.com/blog/20-benefits-of-being-in-gods-word-according-to-psa/.

Simpkins, Daphne. *Kingdom Come: A Mildred Budge Adventure.* Kindle. Quotidian, 2022.

"A Spiritual Woman." Women's Ministries. https://women.adventist.org/a-spiritual-woman.

Vancil, Marilyn. *Beyond the Enneagram: An Invitation to Experience a More Centered Life with God.* New York: Convergent, 2022.

Williams, Susan. "Love that Won't Let Go." That Susan Williams, March 4, 2009. https://www.thatsusanwilliams.com/2009/03/love-that-wont-let-go/.

Wise, Sarah. "Why the Psalms are Important." Emmaus Ministries, March 26, 2020. https://emmausbibleministries.org/blog/2020/3/26/why-the-psalms-are-important.

www.ingramcontent.com/pod-product-compliance
Lightning Source LLC
Chambersburg PA
CBHW050810160426
43192CB00010B/1715